the Soviet Union

Disappeared

How the Soviet Union Disappeared

An Essay on the Causes of Dissolution

Wisła Suraska

Duke University Press Durham and London

1998

© 1998 Duke University Press
All rights reserved
Printed in the United States of America
on acid-free paper ∞
Designed by C. H. Westmoreland
Typeset in Adobe Caslon with Futura Condensed Bold
display by Tseng Information Systems, Inc.
Library of Congress Cataloging-in-Publication Data
appear on the last printed page of this book.

Contents

Foreword

Ten years after the Great Socialist October Revolution of 1917, Will Rogers, the American actor and comedian, said that communism is like prohibition. It's a good idea, but it won't work. We now know that he was right. Since Rogers, several others have claimed that in the long run communism could not work because it went against human nature. But just three decades after Rogers predicted communism's downfall, Americans were scared out of their wits when in 1957 Communist Party Secretary Nikita Khrushchev sent a rocket into space carrying a beeping Sputnik, and then, a few years later, another one carrying a human being. Yury Gagarin returned to Earth, and on the Lenin Mausoleum in Red Square he received a big hug from the leader of the party. Communism seemed to work after all.

The study of communism and the Soviet Union in those days was heavily dominated by the so-called totalitarian model, the "evil empire" that predated President Ronald Reagan by several decades. It was a theoretical construct that suggested complete control of society by the party leadership in the Kremlin. By the time that Khrushchev's Sputnik made its first orbit, however, totalitarianism was lacking in one essential element: the merciless terror that Joseph Stalin used to force both his party and society into submission. Stalin died in 1953. Khrushchev, after he killed Stalin's main henchman, Lavrenti Beria, decided that was enough. In those days Mikhail Gorbachev was a law student at Moscow State University, a budding Komsomol official with, even before Stalin's death, some courage. Shortly before, when Stalin was alive and the so-called Doctors' Plot announced a final round of terror, Gorbachev stood up for a Jewish student who was attacked in class.

It took almost four decades before Gorbachev was presented with the ultimate consequences of Khrushchev's move: the only way to save the Soviet empire was to resort to terror. Gorbachev was a peaceful man, and, anyway, by the time he came to face his ultimate dilemma, the instruments of terror were in the process of disintegration.

All through this period the possibilities for empirical research into communist societies and politics were very limited. This contributed to what Wisła Suraska in her polemical essay calls a "social sciences model-making mania" where labels were more important than content. Social scientists studying communism, she writes, were "chasing their own tail" since the communist regimes themselves, as experiments with Marxist theory, were an offspring of the social sciences. If there was indeed a mania, it was reinforced by the fact that Western students of communism had to work in isolation from scholars in the countries that they studied. Free academic research, after all, was not possible.

That isolation has been broken, and the author of this book personifies the new situation in the study of East-Central European societies. She arrived in the United Kingdom to study at the time of the suppression of Solidarity in Poland, and she participated in heated debates with Sovietologists on the nature of the changes in her society. Raised and trained in Poland, she "could see the insides of the dragon and discover that it was empty" at a time when many Western publics and academics were charmed by Gorbachev's communism "with a human face." Having taken degrees in politics (Oxford), psychology (Jagellonian University, Kraków), and economics (Wroclaw), she made an academic career in the study of postcommunism. She stands for a new generation of postcommunist scholars, the first in many decades to enjoy the privilege of academic freedom and uninhibited discourse with colleagues abroad.

For an old Sovietologist who has had to adapt to the new situation of postcommunism, it is nevertheless striking to see to what extent Wisła Suraska in her argument has made use of the work of his colleagues of the 1960s, 1970s, and 1980s. Indeed, in her interpretation of the collapse of communism, Suraska draws heavily on data and insights provided by the generation of Soviet-

ologists who, like her several decades later, were not satisfied
that the totalitarian model explained very much. They went on a
search for solid facts, and, long before the world had ever heard of
Mikhail Gorbachev, they claimed that the Soviet system worked
less satisfactorily than the totalitarian model suggested. Some of
Suraska's central arguments rest on evidence and interpretation
provided by such pre-Gorbachevian Sovietological research. At
the same time, she shows that many earlier interpretations failed
because they overestimated the degree of central party control
over the USSR's regions and its armed forces.

This book deals with the bloodiest social experiment of the
twentieth century. Indeed, it reflects the sorry fate of millions
of people who had the bad fortune of being turned into guinea
pigs for testing the ideas of Marx, Engels, and Lenin. It seeks
to explain the paradox of communist rulers who claimed to know
that the future was theirs—then surrendered their rule and their
empire without so much as a fight. The Soviet Union had a pro-
liferation of military and police organizations controlled by the
communist party. In few late twentieth-century countries was
the uniform so dominant as in the streets of Minsk, Moscow, or
Magadan. During the last two years of Gorbachev's rule, rumors
of military coups and coming civil war were the order of the
day. The vested interests were not going to give up without a
fight. And yet, in August 1991, the endgame was triggered by a
miserable coup attempt of a handful of men-from-the-past who
had lost touch with reality. Four months later the Soviet Union
was over. On the day that he abdicated the saddened Gorbachev
wrote to "Dear Margaret" Thatcher that "this is not an easy day
for me." As Huib Hendrikse, one of the most perceptive Dutch
Sovietologists later wrote, the Soviet state had collapsed "like a
dinosaur with a brain haemorrhage."

Dragon or dinosaur? In the end, no overpowering external force
had been necessary. The control center had basic flaws, and the
nerve system was too primitive for such an unwieldy body poli-
tic. Many books have since been written on the causes of the
collapse, not the least in Russia itself. The academic discussion

on this century's gruesome experiment in social engineering and on its inglorious end will no doubt continue. In the confusion of tongues that has been triggered by the Soviet downfall, Suraska's essay stands out as a towering example of a clear thinking, based on the firm foundations of solid historical knowledge and creative theoretical interpretation.

John Löwenhardt
Alexander Nove Professor of Russian and East European Studies,
The University of Glasgow

Prologue

Among a multitude of historical facts there are some, and those by much the majority, which prove nothing more than that they are facts. There are others that may be useful in drawing a partial conclusion, whereby a philosopher may be enabled to judge the motives of an action, or some peculiar features in a character; these relate only to single links of the chain. Those whose influence extends throughout the whole system, and which are so intimately connected as to give motion to the springs of action, are very rare. —Edward Gibbon, *Essai sur l'étude de la littérature*[1]

That multinational empires are doomed in the age of democracy and nationalism is a simple proposition and, by itself, a plausible enough explanation of the demise of the Soviet Union. But history also shows how enduring imperial rule can be, even when its disintegration is apparent. The moribund Habsburg empire was shaken by nationalist discontent throughout the second half of the nineteenth century, but it disintegrated only in 1918 after it found itself on the losing side in the Great War. An earlier example, the Ottoman empire, also shows the tenacity of established imperial rule; it took more than a hundred years of internecine wars and dickering between the Great Powers to spell its end. Furthermore, Soviet power was much more extensive. A special term—totalitarianism—had to be coined to distinguish it from the other regimes. Unlike the Ottoman rulers, who tolerated diversity among peoples under their rule, the Soviet Union maintained a high degree of ideological, political, and economic uniformity, not only within its own borders, but also among its satellites. Once introduced at enormous cost, such a system was not easy to break up. Indeed, even the greatest skeptics did not expect the Soviet Union to end in such a fortuitous way.

Confronted with the avalanche of changes in Eastern Europe since 1989, we tend to forget what the Soviet Union was like back in 1985. At that time the newly elected Soviet leader, Mikhail Gorbachev, inherited a primitive but entrenched administrative machinery—the party apparatus. By and large, Soviet society was docile and kept under tight rein by an elaborate system of indoctrination and intimidation. Last but not least, there was a powerful army and the most extensive apparatus of political police in the world. True, the economy was slowing down, and this fact, combined with a technological race that had already been lost, would have had serious consequences for the future. However, none of these things explains the speed and profundity of the collapse. A growing consensus has developed to the effect that, were it not for Gorbachev and his perestroika, the Soviet Union would still be in a formidable international position, perhaps even with the Warsaw Pact intact.

The importance of the Gorbachev phenomenon in bringing about the fall of the Soviet Union reaffirms romantic views of the role of the individual in history. Since the events that he inspired have been truly millenarian, his personality and motives tend to be idealized. Yet little investigative scholarship has focused on Gorbachev and his career. The cult that he enjoys outside Russia is in itself an interesting phenomenon. Even many American writers, who often excel in uncovering critically important historical details about their own political leaders, take Gorbachev's official biography at face value.

Gorbachev's cult was initiated by the Left, who expected him to make the Soviet system work and fulfill its initial promise. In this sense some Western scholarship on perestroika was heir to an earlier tradition of "intellectual pilgrimage" from the Stalinist era, which culminated in what Paul Hollander called a "grotesque and embarrassing chapter in Western intellectual-political history."[2] I refer to the cult of Stalin transplanted from the Soviet Union to the Western world of letters. Yet the appeal of Gorbachev's millennium was much wider, since its connotations were less radical, than those of Stalinist partisanship. Although Gorbachev preached some kind of revolution, his tenets were garnished with the postmodern lingo of globalism and interdependence.

After the Soviet Union's great failure, Gorbachev became a more interesting figure to the political Right. Unlike the Left, the Rightists saw the coming of the millennium in the collapse of the Soviet Union rather than in its preservation. They began to see Gorbachev as the representative of Russian idealism striving to reform an ossified empire. Neither Gorbachev's personality nor his motives, however, were necessarily as majestic as were the consequences of his deeds. While Gorbachev's personality awaits a comprehensive analysis, an attempt is made in these pages to place him in the context of his own generation. I will argue in chapter 1 that Gorbachev's generation was already cut off from Russian pre-Revolutionary traditions and mores; it was the first Soviet generation to have grown up under the Stalinist regime.

Another character is typical of Russian culture, a "holy fool," who by chance overcomes the dragon. Perhaps such a portrayal of Gorbachev's role in demolishing Soviet communism is more accurate than other descriptions. But was the dragon he set out to kill, the one he ended up slaying? Lengthy analyses describe Gorbachev's tactical maneuvers between various forces of the fragmented Soviet center in his efforts to stay on top of whatever wave prevailed. A typical conclusion is that he was a great tactician without much in the way of a strategy. This view implies that Gorbachev had no clear political objectives other than his desire to stay in power, which might, in fact, be true in the last year or so of his rule. To say the same about the first half of his tenure, however, would be as preposterous as the opposite view that perestroika was altogether unavoidable.

This book is an inquiry into the dynamics of the Soviet collapse. Three perspectives will be employed to examine the mechanisms of Soviet disintegration: horizontal-territorial, vertical-institutional, and international. Such distinctions are useful beyond analytical purposes. Almost simultaneously, the empire's dissolution proceeded territorially, institutionally, and internationally, thus making the Soviet drama all the more spectacular. While the Union republics, one after another, proclaimed their independence, the Soviet "sphere of interest" in Central Europe was rapidly shrinking, Germany was being unified within the North Atlantic Treaty Organization, and the erstwhile Soviet satellites were leaving the Warsaw Pact. In the face of this collapse, the army was reluctant to engage in emergency measures required to save the integrity of the Soviet state. These developments, to some extent, occurred as a chain reaction. Nevertheless, each strand of disintegration—territorial, institutional, and imperial— had its own causes and dynamics inherent in perestroika. That is why they are discussed in three separate chapters 2, 3, and 4.

Several detailed accounts of perestroika exist, its timing, the personal background of its architects, and the general climate in which it developed. Nevertheless, to explain the motives of the main actors and the meaning of their actions, researchers often have made some assumptions that are difficult to sustain. For example, Gorbachev's reformist zeal is most often explained in terms of economic necessity. A survey of the policies of perestroika reveals, however, that their main thrust was not economic —it was political. Gorbachev dismantled the Soviet political and administrative institutions, leaving the principle of central planning in the economy virtually intact. The nationalized and centrally planned economy was perhaps the last item of socialist faith that Gorbachev never forfeited as the Soviet leader; this was what he meant when he described himself as a communist. Although it was not realistic to expect the Soviet economy to work with its political and administrative structures pulled from under its feet, the Soviet economic breakdown still appears to be the *outcome* of political reform rather than its cause.

Another popular assumption challenged in this study is that Gorbachev's initial intention was to curb the power of the Soviet state by means of democratic reforms. The analysis in chapter 2 will show that, as the regime that he inherited already was partly fragmented, his objective was to concentrate power rather than to disperse it. In this connection a theory of patrimonial regression is offered that explains both Stalin's and Gorbachev's policies as "revolutions from above," designed to cope with the typical predicament of despotic regimes—their tendency toward territorial fragmentation. This phenomenon has been best summarized by Charles Tilly as a reductio ad absurdum: a large empire "goes through a continuous cycle of building up power in its peripheral units only to see those who have direct access to that power turn it to their own ends and against the central structure."[3]

Paradoxically, the centrally planned economy furthered the territorial fragmentation of the Soviet state, since it was inextricably connected to the arbitrary nature of the regime. When economic resources dwindled, Moscow became increasingly dependent on its territorial apparatus for their mobilization; what else, in the absence of markets, could provide a modicum of control over wasteful industrial enterprises? The problem, however, was how to keep regional leaders loyal and responsive, that is, how to prevent them from building regional empires of their own through control of the resources that they supervised.

Democratization was Gorbachev's weapon against the centers of baronial power entrenched not only in the non-Russian republics but also in the purely Russian regions. He considered his contest a two-corner game, with the public likely to take his side against the corrupt apparatchiks. But when a ruling elite splits and the public is given a choice between fighting factions, it also becomes an actor, thus turning a two-corner game into a three-corner contest. This, in turn, spells the end of dictatorship. The process was depicted earlier by Alexander Stromas in his "second pivot" theory, although the pivots that he considered were different from those suggested here.

Gorbachev clearly overestimated his capacity to concentrate power that had diffused from Moscow over the period of stagnation. Confronted with the consequences of perestroika in the summer of 1990, he sought reconciliation with the aggravated apparatchiks at the final Soviet Party Congress. At this stage, however, mobilization at the periphery acquired a momentum of it own and was impossible to stop by peaceful means. Yet the new conservative coalition formed by Gorbachev in the autumn of 1990 might have had a chance, if only the center held. But it did not. In fact, the most lethal conflict was personal rather than national; the emergence of Boris Yeltsin as the new charismatic leader vested with popular legitimacy left Gorbachev no choice but to return to the traditional Soviet power base, that is, to the forces of coercion. But the army remained equivocal and was continuing to consider its options, even at the height of the crisis.

The army was alienated by perestroika and especially by the New Thinking, but this alone cannot fully explain why it stood by as the Soviet state was coming apart. To understand this—and how the New Thinking was possible in the first place—some historical perspective is required. In chapter 3 a history of the long-festering conflict between the KGB and the army is recapitulated. I try to show how, in the course of a contest between these two pillars of the Soviet regime, all other considerations, including Soviet imperial interests and even the sacrosanct interests of the party, became secondary. In effect, the army lost this struggle in the spring of 1987, when the entire military command was fired in the aftermath of the Rust affair (named after a German youth who landed his Cessna in Red Square).

The KGB victory was Pyrrhic, however, as was revealed during the August coup in 1990. In the final confrontation with the forces unleashed by perestroika, the KGB failed to control the course of events because of the army's lack of support. The military itself may now be having second thoughts about its equivocal attitude toward the August coup, as it struggles at the end of the nineties for its own survival amid the debris of empire.

The final blow came from a radical change in Soviet foreign policy, which led to the dissolution of the outer empire, thereby undermining the Soviet government's imperial legitimacy within its own borders. What made Gorbachev give up his key strategic position in Central Europe? This is by far the most mysterious part of the story. Never before had an empire made such profound concessions to its adversaries, as Germany and the United States were considered in the Soviet traditional security doctrine.

Gorbachev's choices in the twilight of his rule concerning the unification of Germany are examined and given a new interpretation in chapter 4. The reversal of Soviet foreign policy is attributed to the Soviet elite's changing perceptions of the outside world. To understand this change, one must examine a peculiar phenomenon—the grip of post-Marxist and postmodern ideas on sections of the new Soviet elite. The channels through which these new ideas found their way into Gorbachev's ideological team are described in chapter 2, and their role in the dismantling of traditional Soviet foreign policy is considered in chapter 4.

The debate among social scientists concerning the collapse of the Soviet Union has proceeded along divisions long established in Soviet studies. Conservatives see the totalitarian model vindicated, since the Soviet regime proved, after all, impervious to reform. The revisionists, in turn, see the same model refuted by the fact that reforms, whatever their outcome, nevertheless took place. At the same time, the defenders of modernization theory see the growth of civil society in the Soviet Union as responsible for the Union's demise. To be sure, no single perspective or theory can explain a subject as vast as the collapse of an empire. What is confusing is not so much the variety of approaches as the difficulty of aggregating results across various schools of thought.

One reason for this confusion is that while searching for the causes of the Soviet collapse, the social sciences appear to be chasing their own tails. Communist regimes were themselves a peculiar offspring of social sciences; they provided an opportunity to apply scientific paradigms to a living society. Many social scientists were conceptual insiders of the Soviet Union, perhaps even more so than the ordinary people who lived there. Social theory, in the guise of scientific ideology, provided a convenient framework for explaining Soviet political and economic decisions as well as Soviet military doctrines, but it also authored a most effective critique—the theory of totalitarianism. This theory undermined the claim of communist regimes to moral superiority; just as industrial entrepreneurs in the West were challenged with the shame of being capitalists and exploiters, so many communist apparatchiks found themselves affected by the image of a totalitarian state. Thereby, they lost the high moral ground, even before losing the political battle.

The power of social theory to define moral standards and thereby to influence the real world often equals that of religion. This fact, however, does not make such theory any more valid as a scientific model. In particular, when it comes to explaining the failure of the Soviet regime, Marxist theory on which it was founded turns out to be least suitable as an instrument of inquiry. It will take some time, however, before the social sciences are released from the Procrustean bed of Marxist eschatology.

The intellectual response to the collapse of communism, instead of offering an across-the-board revision of social science's leading paradigms, proclaims the end of any further development in social and political theory altogether. Such a conclusion is difficult to accept. After all, the features and fortunes of communist regimes provide us with the empirical material required for a reassessment of ideas on which they were founded. In chapter 5 the major models employed to explain the Soviet regime will be reconsidered against the story of its breakup. A preliminary attempt at a synthesis of what is left of these theories after the fall of the Soviet Union is offered in chapter 6.

Chapter 1

The First Soviet

Generation

Bertrand Russell saw the major weakness of the rising dictatorships of the 1930s in the fact that the system of organized lying upon which they depended kept their followers out of touch with reality and therefore put them at a disadvantage in comparison to those who knew the facts. George Orwell commented gloomily on this piece of liberal optimism: "it does not prove that the slave society at which the dictators are aiming will be unstable. It is quite easy to imagine a state in which the ruling caste deceive their followers without deceiving themselves."[1]

In the case of the Soviet Union, Orwell got it right as far as Stalin's elite was concerned. Those who were responsible for the terror could deceive the public without themselves losing their grip on reality. The regime was, in fact, relatively stable as long as they—the Brezhnev generation—stayed in power. But Russell's optimism was vindicated by the next generation of Soviet political leaders. Those who, like Mikhail Gorbachev, had grown up under mature Stalinism fell victim to organized lying and thus parted company with reality.

In the following chapters various structural causes and mechanisms behind the breakup of the Soviet Union will be discussed. But the regime's features and functioning do not tell the full story of its collapse. To understand the particular way in which that happened, we have to look more closely at the reformers themselves and their intellectual and moral makeups. The main argument here is that the Gorbachev elite set out to reform a regime that they knew little about because of this regime's elaborate mechanisms of deception. Furthermore, their knowledge of the liberal democratic institutions that they strove to install at home was likewise seriously flawed. Specifically, I will argue that the notion of democracy which Gorbachev's radical advisers took from the Western social sciences made them seriously overestimate their ability to control the democratic process.

Since Gorbachev's personality plays an important part in the interpretations proposed below, a few words about sources that discuss him are in order. Considering his role in bringing about the end of the Soviet Union, it is surprising how casually Gorbachev's biography has been dealt with by writers on perestroika, even by those who have produced penetrating portraits of other perestroika personalities. Few neutral descriptions of Gorbachev have been published. The most friendly account so far has been given by Archie Brown, whose purpose was to defend him as a person and to exonerate his record as a statesman.[2] It seems that Brown has been more successful at defending the person than the record. The most critical picture of the last leader of the Soviet Union has been painted by his chief of staff, the former editor of *Pravda,* Valery Boldin, who was involved in the August coup.[3] Interesting portraits on the early period of Gorbachev's career were offered by some Russian émigrés.[4]

I have examined numerous interviews with Gorbachev and his collaborators as well as the many memoirs. Not all of these relatively recent sources are of equal value. First, books where Gorbachev appears as author ought to be treated as official Soviet documents, carefully prepared by his specialized staff for political purposes. Gorbachev's *Perestroika* is a good example of such an exercise in public relations, addressed mainly to the Western reader.[5] Gorbachev himself was a diligent writer from the early years of his career. His chief of staff, Boldin, recalls that he "loved to get into print. With him, it was a veritable passion. . . ."[6] Nevertheless, years of writing for official party purposes left its mark on his style, which is hardly attractive. In his memoirs, as well as in his earlier account of the August coup, he also appears unreliable as a reporter and less than diligent as an analyst.[7] Although Gorbachev has been a good communicator, a fact on which both his friends and foes agree, it seems that writing is not his medium.

Several memoirs have appeared by leading figures of the perestroika period.[8] Most of them are written in a wooden language and are as stiff and featureless as their authors. On the other hand, the memoirs of newcomers from the democratic opposition constitute a pleasant change, especially the one written by Anatoly Sobchak.[9] Boris Yeltsin's memoirs also belong in this category;[10] although he was hardly a newcomer on the Soviet political stage, Yeltsin was the first among the Soviet elite to have forebodings about the coming era of mass democracy. A comparison of his memoirs with Gorbachev's makes it easier to understand why Yeltsin won the contest with the Soviet public. Even though one may guess that both men relied heavily on ghostwriters, Yeltsin's ghost clearly belongs to the new era, whereas Gorbachev's preserves the Newspeak touch.

Among the foreign journalists who reported on perestroika from the Soviet Union, the most complex portrait of Gorbachev was provided by David Remnick, the New York Times correspondent at the time.[11] Remnick also reveals how difficult it was to conduct independent research on Gorbachev's past. Journalists interested in this subject were offered a carefully organized tour from which it was difficult for them to diverge.[12] Such limits were discarded after Gorbachev ceased to be the Soviet leader. For example, in the valuable collection of interviews presented by David Pryce-Jones, Gorbachev's collaborators speak much more freely than on earlier occasions about themselves and their boss.[13] My own "primary source" was Victor Gayduk, who came to serve on Gorbachev's staff from the publishing unit of the Central Committee, Beloy Progres; he offered valuable insight into the channels through which new ideas from the West flowed into the bastion of Soviet orthodoxy.

In this chapter the accounts given by Gorbachev's friends and foes are drawn upon, as they convey what seems to me a very similar picture. Even though this picture is far from comprehensive, its features may improve our understanding of the motives behind some of Gorbachev's decisions that have changed the face of Europe.

The Children of Stalinist Society

Shortly before Brezhnev's death the average age of Politburo members was over seventy years. The golden rule of the stability of cadres, which Brezhnev had practiced for about two decades, meant that the highest officials died in office. From 1982 until 1985 four members of the Politburo, that is, 30 percent of the highest governing body, passed away. The ruling oligarchy was virtually disappearing, its prestige turning to ridicule with each state funeral. But, as Walter Laqueur observed, "ridicule doesn't kill in Russia."[14] Only at the initiative of Foreign Minister Andrei Gromyko, who best understood the damage done to the superpower's international standing by its aging leadership, did the Politburo finally abandon the seniority rule, and in March 1985 the fifty-four-year-old Mikhail Sergeyevich Gorbachev was chosen for the top position. Soon afterward the members of the new generation, then in their forties and early fifties, began forcing out the Brezhnevite gerontocracy at all levels of the party and state apparatus.[15] The machinery of advancement in the Soviet power structure, clogged for decades, moved on again.

University education became more common among the Gorbachev elite than it had ever been before. This generation of apparatchiks was also the first to gain promotion in the relatively peaceful era of the 1960s. For that reason, they were expected by some Western observers to be bolder than previous leaderships about structural reforms.[16] Other observers were more skeptical. Severyn Bialer pointed out that members of the generation in waiting had been carefully selected by their superiors and well-domesticated in the existing structures during more than two decades of service.[17] Both skeptics and hopefuls were in for a surprise. The new generation did make a difference — and a much greater difference than anticipated. But the features that had led observers to hope for change also made this generation singularly unsuited to reform the Soviet political system.

For all their diplomas, the political elite born in the 1930s belonged to the first Soviet generation that had learned history from Stalinist textbooks. The historical sciences in the Soviet Union were in the grip of Stalinist dogma well into the 1980s (even since then, change in educational standards has been slow to come).[18] While watching the debate on Stalinism in the Soviet Union under perestroika, Walter Laqueur had the distinct impression that "the present generation of Soviet leaders knows little about the historical facts of their party and country . . . [they] may genuinely believe what they were taught when they were younger men . . . ."[19]

When Gorbachev called for a revision of party history that would deal openly with Stalin's years, he did not seem fully aware of the possible consequences that such openness would have on the legitimacy of his own government.[20] In 1988 he said in an interview with *L'Humanité* that there was no such thing as Stalinism; it was a concept thought up to discredit the Soviet Union and socialism.[21] He might well have meant it.

This is not to say that Gorbachev and others around him did not know about the atrocities of the Stalinist era. After all, many of them had childhood memories of their own parents being persecuted. Later on, as members of the inner circle, they had much better access than others to party secrets and foreign literature. What was lacking, therefore, was not knowledge of the facts but the criteria on which to judge them and from which to draw moral as well as practical conclusions.

Growing up under mature Stalinism meant, among other things, an estrangement from pre-Revolutionary moral notions. The means such as family, church, and community through which a moral code was transmitted to children had been broken by the time this generation entered school. The Stalinist terror deeply penetrated even the most intimate of human relations; parents were afraid to talk to their children, who were presented in schools with role models such as Pavka Morozov, the boy who denounced his parents to the security services as "enemies of the people," thus causing their deportation. Children's moral notions were shaped entirely by teachers who were either Stalinist zealots themselves or under the strict control of such people. This meant a rupture in the transmission of moral norms from one generation to another.

As one of Gorbachev's advisers, Yuri Afanasyev, recalled from his childhood, mass deportations, even those affecting his own family, were not experienced as "grief or tragedy"; they were part of everyday life. Hardly anyone dared to express criticism of the regime in front of children: "We never heard any conversations about Stalin and I had no doubts about him."[22] Eduard Shevardnadze's mother refused to answer any of his questions when his father was taken away; his most vivid memory of that time was being stigmatized as a son of an enemy of the people.[23]

The experience of being branded for a parent's "betrayal" was typical for Gorbachev's generation, and its impact on the future personal development of those who suffered it should not be underestimated. The children who lost their parents in the Stalinist purges had themselves embraced the cult of Stalin with an unprecedented zeal; after all, this was the only safe haven left to those whose childhood world was turned upside-down. However, no matter how hard they tried to show their devotion to the new doctrine, their loss of personal security and confidence was permanent. This, in turn, fed their attachment to dogma. Many people from this generation refuse to talk about Stalinist crimes other than to say that times were difficult and things were complicated. Even nowadays many do not understand what all the fuss is about. Whatever their knowledge of Stalinist atrocities, moral outrage is often missing from their recollections. On the contrary, Stalinism provided Soviet society with its own causes and virtues, the only ones that post-Revolutionary generations had ever known.

In the Antechambers of Power

Apart from age and education, two other features distinguished the Gorbachev elite from their predecessors: their early start in the business of politics and the longer waiting time that they faced for promotion to more responsible posts. If the Brezhnevites included a significant number of "co-opted specialists" who came to political positions from their respective fields (most often from industry), the Gorbachevites had much less work experience outside the political apparatus and more frequently their careers originated in the KGB and MVD.[24] They began their political careers early on, often in their teens, as Komsomol organizers. After graduation, they would go to work in Komsomol provincial committees and wait for promotion to the lower ranks of the party apparatus, frequently in the same province. The earlier generation had moved quickly to responsible political posts emptied by Stalin's purges. This generation had to mount the hierarchy of power laboriously, step by step.

The early start and long waiting time in the antechambers of power created a peculiar blend of qualities. The Gorbachev generation had become better-educated and more sophisticated than its predecessors, but it also was more detached from life outside the political apparatus, accustomed to privilege but not to personal responsibility. At the time when members of that generation entered the provincial apparatus, the style of local leadership in the Soviet Union began to change. By Brezhnev's time the peripatetic party secretaries of the Stalinist era had entrenched themselves in local patronage networks. The mechanisms for selecting political leaders were different in both periods. If Stalin's revolution from above gave career opportunities to dynamic—even if ruthless—individuals, the Brezhnev machinery eliminated personalities with any measure of autonomy and promoted only the faithful.

The elite that Gorbachev brought to the wheel helped him break through the entrenched Soviet establishment with the energies accumulated during the long wait for power. In the end, however, the new generation proved incapable of keeping the regime's vital structures in working order. Its lack of the Stalinist experience proved to be a liability rather than an asset in this new assignment.

The Soviet "Rural Gentry"

Charles Fairbanks has pointed to yet another significant difference between the Gorbachev and Brezhnev elites.[25] Unlike the Brezhnevites, who for the most part were upwardly mobile sons of peasants and workers, many perestroika personalities came from the regime's "aristocracy," old Bolshevik families, often from rural areas. Gorbachev himself grew up in a kolkhoz (collective farm) that had been organized and chaired by his grandfather. Most Gorbachev biographies show him as a "perfect Soviet boy," helping his father work the kolkhoz fields in his spare time, even getting the Order of the Red Banner of Labor at age sixteen.

Such an idyllic image conceals the almost daily confrontations that Gorbachev must have faced with local hostilities left behind by brutal collectivization, which wiped out one-third of his native province's population. Indeed, his own family was torn apart. While his maternal grandfather was forcing peasants into collective farms, his paternal grandfather was deported, and nearly half of his family perished for transgressions against the new system. When it was the turn of the "little Stalins" of the Soviet countryside to fill the gulags, his maternal grandfather was arrested on charges of Trotskyism, but he survived the persecution and returned home.

Fairbanks has concluded that risks inherent until recent years in representing the regime in the Russian village produced a higher proportion of idealists among the progeny of the communist "rural gentry" than among their urban counterparts.[26] That may be so, but some other circumstances should be accounted for as well. One difference between the kolkhoz officials and the rest of the village was that the former did not have to starve. "Gorbachev's family were living in their own house on their own soil. They always had enough to eat," said Gorbachev's high school sweetheart in describing the difference between her self-confident beau and others like herself.[27]

Not starving, not having been forced to resettle, these were the tangible benefits of representing the regime in the village. Further, growing up as a perfect Soviet boy at that time also meant learning very early on about the primacy of politics over all other considerations in one's career. Komsomol militants of the Stalinist era could exercise considerable powers over their colleagues and teachers, and they sometimes did so ruthlessly. Young Misha belonged to this group. "He was fearless for someone of that age," Gorbachev's classmate recalls. "Once he was so angry at one teacher he said 'Do you want to keep your teaching certificate?'"[28]

Gorbachev was advancing in the Komsomol hierarchy at the law school of Moscow University in the early fifties, the time of the anti-Semitic witch-hunt. This is one fragment of Gorbachev's biography that has troubled more sympathetic writers. Archie Brown vouches for Gorbachev that he "did not . . . engage in witch-hunts, although he doubtless did not deviate from the 'general line' of the party."[29] But he must have been active to become a member of the Moscow University party committee only a year or so after becoming a full member of the CPSU. One law school student, Lev Yudovich, recalls that Gorbachev actively supported Stalinist policies and "took a hard line during discussions of people's personal affairs." Another student remembers that "he was the plague of the law school. We feared Misha. . . . When he walked by, everybody stopped talking."[30] Gorbachev's choice of Lublyanka for his internship, although it fell through because of post-Stalinist changes already under way, was nevertheless telling as to the direction that he hoped his career would take.[31]

To judge the Stalinist beginnings of Gorbachev's career according to present standards would be anachronistic. As the third generation of a family with communist traditions, he was born in the Stalinist era and had known no other. In this respect he was typical rather than exceptional for the so-called post-Stalinist generation, which was formed almost exclusively by Stalinist institutions, brainwashed in schools, Pioneer organizations, and the Komsomol. In its upbringing and education, this generation encountered few challenges to official doctrine.

The Komsomol militants of the early 1950s are sometimes called a "deceived generation," indoctrinated in their early youth, only to become disenchanted later in life. Yet the nature of the "deception" was ambivalent. The revelations of Nikita Khrushchev's secret speech in 1956 were by no means unknown to the high-ranking Komsomol *aktiv*. That Gorbachev himself was clearly aware of discrepancies between official propaganda and real life we know from the testimony of his roommate, Zdenek Mlynar.[32] To this generation, what was new in Khrushchev's address to the Twentieth Party Congress was that the things and people extolled by the party as worthy of the highest admiration were being politically and morally condemned by the same party.[33] This was the second time that the world was turned upside-down for the young Gorbachev and his peers.

The message of the post-Stalinist thaw was easier to understand and embrace by those who remembered the pre-Revolutionary moral order. On the next generation, for whom Stalinist atrocities had been an everyday childhood experience, one apparently accepted by grown-ups, the moral dimension of Khrushchev's revelations might have been lost. The post-Stalinist thaw left Stalinist progeny in a state of confusion. Yet the new norms were even more difficult to accept, since they undermined the very basis of already established career prospects. These younger careerists had to start again from scratch, learning the new rules of the political game and at much lower ranks than they had expected.

The end of Stalinism also meant a halt to Gorbachev's career. His party contacts from the university must have appeared useless since he was not offered a job in Moscow. "De-Stalinisation confused him and pulled the rug from under his feet. For him, it was a real political catastrophe."[34] His chief of staff also remembers that Gorbachev must have been hurt deeply by the fact that he was not offered a job in Moscow. "He would harp on this point relentlessly."[35] Gorbachev had to take his newlywed wife back to Stavropol, where he started his career anew from the bottom of the provincial hierarchy as assistant head of the propaganda section of the Komsomol's territorial committee. He was stuck in the Stavropol Komsomol apparatus for another six years, already growing too old for the youth organization. Only the arrival in the province of a new first secretary opened up his career prospects.

Fyodor Kulakov came to Stavropol from Moscow, where he had been a minister in the Russian Republic's government, had fallen from grace with Khrushchev, and had been exiled to the provinces. He was an intelligent man with ideas of his own.[36] In the four years of Kulakov's provincial leadership, he introduced several new projects, experimented with the wasteful kolkhoz system, constructed irrigation channels, etc. Gorbachev became Kulakov's right-hand man, dutifully following the demanding work schedule set by his boss and mentor. He advanced quickly, first to the position of secretary for agriculture and then, after Kulakov was called back to Moscow, he took over his post of first secretary. Here, Gorbachev's career in all likelihood would have ended had it not been for the special quality of spring waters in his province, which attracted some top dignitaries from Moscow, the KGB chairman, Yuri Andropov, among them.

To win the trust of the suspicious and withdrawn Andropov was no mean achievement, and it was the act that decided Gorbachev's future. Andropov already had made a bid for the succession after Brezhnev and was building up his personal following in the provinces. The bright, ambitious Gorbachev, with his discreet and obliging demeanor, was the perfect man for him. Andropov became Gorbachev's next patron. "We owe everything to Yuri Vladimirovich," confessed Raisa Gorbachev. He arranged Gorbachev's promotion to the CC Secretariat and Politburo membership, and finally, after Andropov's ascension to the top position of general secretary, shortly before he died he anointed Gorbachev his successor.[37]

Thus, Gorbachev's career was made for him by two powerful patrons, both strong-willed, independent, and gifted men, who were attracted by his discreet manners, intelligence, and excellent understanding of what was expected of him. These qualities also would help him get along with Brezhnevite gerontocrats when he was elected the youngest member of the Politburo in 1978. Gorbachev had won their trust by suggesting the rehabilitation of old Stalinists like Lazar Kaganovich and Georgy Malenkov, and making an occasional anti-Semitic remark about Andrei Sakharov's wife.[38] After six years in the Politburo, Gorbachev had created such a familiar and benign image of himself that Gromyko felt obliged to stress, while recommending him for the highest posts, that "under his nice smile Gorbachev hid the teeth of iron." Gorbachev's Politburo cronies, however, certainly did not share this perception.

The Unhinged Generation

Who, in reality, was Mikhail Sergeyevich Gorbachev? A Stalinist vigilante feared by his classmates? A Khrushchevite enthusiast diligently active on agricultural improvements in Stavropol province? A Brezhnevite apparatchik, working inside the Politburo on behalf of his patron, who happened to be the head of the KGB? A petty anti-Semite? A pragmatist, with whom the British prime minister, Margaret Thatcher, "could do business"? A great reformer whose charisma impressed even sophisticated Leningrad intellectuals like Anatoly Sobchak? He could have been all of these things as well as none of them since he was, above all, a great performer.

Gorbachev became involved with acting during his high school years, and he even considered a career in the theater.[39] His later collaborators also noticed in him "a kind of performing artist's delight in seeing himself as the initiator of reform and democratization."[40] The prime minister, Valentin Pavlov, described Gorbachev as "an extremely talented actor, in the sense that actors can give a thoroughly convincing performance of understanding things about which they have no real conception."[41] Unlike other apparatchiks, Gorbachev used to have a good rapport with his audience. Sobchak remembered that what most attracted him to Gorbachev was his ability to answer sensitive questions in a straightforward, reliable manner.[42]

Perhaps Gorbachev was sincere when talking to democrats and only performing for the Brezhnev Politburo loyalists to convince them that he was their man. Or he might have changed over time. The point is that he had the rare skill of winning the trust of even the most distrustful people, men and women who were diverse in their worldviews and expectations. At least at the beginning of his career, he had confidence "in his ability to convince anyone of anything."[43] It might have been Gorbachev's knack for exhortation that made German Chancellor Helmut Kohl describe him as "a propagandist of the Goebbels type."[44] This unfortunate remark made in 1986 did not stop Kohl from successfully applying his own powers of persuasion a few years later when he managed to convince Gorbachev that the unification of Germany on terms set by the Western Allies was in the best interest of the Soviet Union.

Hypocrisy is not a strong indictment when directed at a politician, but to be a hypocrite one needs some fixed principles to forfeit in the first place. Gorbachev, like many others of his generation, seemed to lack such a code. Brought up under untrammeled Stalinism, which was first denounced and then reintroduced in a trimmed-down version (though never openly admitted), Gorbachev and his peers had become an "unhinged generation." They developed a floating conscience, easy to refurbish for each passing patron. What might have made Gorbachev a sincere performer was his career path as a faithful follower of powerful patrons, that is, the permanent second-in-command. The problems started when he became the first-in-charge, with no one to report to, a supreme boss all to himself.

The outward appearances of Gorbachev's marriage also identified him as an externally rather than internally guided person. Raisa's role in the rise and fall of her husband should not be underestimated. An ambitious and intelligent woman, she seemed to wield a strong influence over Gorbachev in all matters, including the day-to-day business of government.[45] "When Gorbachev came home after work . . . (the guards told me about this)," Boris Yeltsin has written, "Raisa used to meet him at the door and take him for a walk . . . [then] he would tell her his whole day, literally by minute. Gorbachev's wife was not just informed; she was given a total briefing."[46] Gorbachev did not hide the weight he gave to his wife's advice; he called her "the head of the family's party cell."[47] She seemed to be a perfect political wife, but her social prominence did not sit well with Soviet custom. Gorbachev's open devotion to her reflected badly on his political image throughout the country.

Nevertheless, the Gorbachevs abroad were always a resounding success. The *New York Times,* for example, is typical in describing one of their visits to the United States: "there was a murmur of excitement and the Gorbachevs were entering the room, and it was as if royalty had appeared in our midst. . . ."[48] Gorbachev's chief media adviser, Leonid Kravchenko, observed that his boss became a "hostage to his international popularity."[49] It seems, though, that more than plain vanity affected Gorbachev's conduct on the international stage. He had been admitted to the club of Western leaders as an equal, or so he thought, and he tried his best to live up to the other leaders' expectations, as he had done with his former patrons. This was a question of loyalty.

To be sure, Gorbachev's new loyalty was somehow misplaced, and it prompted accusations of selling out from the then Soviet and now Russian hard-liners. But such a sell-out cannot be considered in its ordinary sense. Rather, it was Gorbachev's lifelong habit to deliver what was expected of him by the powerful. Fulfilling expectations of his former patrons was how he made it to the top in the first place. In particular, the authoritative figure of Helmut Kohl, the German chancellor, might have filled a gap left by Gorbachev's dead mentors.

Patricians and Bumpkins

Ernest Gellner pointed to the conspicuous lack of an affirmed theory behind perestroika and he called Gorbachev's reform "a Reformation without a Bible, an Enlightenment without an *Encyclopédie*."[50] He saw the reason for this lack in a communist ideology that had lost its initial messianic zeal and was even tacitly recognized as a failure by the reformers. But replacing communism by any counterfaith was impossible without undermining the institution that was supposed to carry out reforms, that is, the Communist Party of the Soviet Union. The problem was indeed intractable and led to a deadly stalemate in which the party could carry out neither its day-to-day business nor the reforms. However, perestroika was not entirely without its encyclopedists and their source of inspiration can also be identified; the bible of Gorbachev's reforms consisted of post-Marxist and postmodern ideas already prevalent in the Western world of letters.

Several myths have been created about Gorbachev's ideological team. They received a collective name—*shestidesyatniki*—from the early 1960s, a short-lived period of thaw in the Soviet Union. The post-Stalinist thaw gave rise to waves of revisionism in Poland and later on in Czechoslovakia, whereas in the Soviet Union revisionism amounted to no more than a rivulet authored by the *shestidesyatniki*. Revisionism, Soviet-style, had its nest in the CC department for contacts with communist parties, a vestige of the once-powerful Comintern. Like its predecessor, it was by tradition closely tied to the KVD-KGB. In the late 1950s and early 1960s the department was chaired by an old Comintern hand, Otto Kuusinen, who also brought in his protégé, Yuri Andropov, after Andropov distinguished himself as Soviet ambassador in Budapest during the 1956 Hungarian uprising.

The department performed the traditional Comintern function of an "ideological police" in the communist world. Kuusinen and Andropov gathered around themselves a group of intellectuals with the task of revising *The Foundations of Marxism-Leninism* for the post-Stalinist era.[51] The work proceeded amid rambling discourses on abstract principles, very much in the old Bolshevik tradition of high intellectual debates (which once humiliated Stalin so much that he felt compelled to take tutorials in dialectical materialism to hold his own in Lenin's Politburo). Such intellectual exchanges disappeared, together with their protagonists, during the Great Purge, only to be re-created by Andropov's intellectuals, who still remember his department as an "oasis of free thinking." This relative openness would be difficult to discern, though, from the outcome of their work; the revised *Foundations* was hard to distinguish from its previous version. According to one of the authors of those revisions, the crucial change was in the definition of the Soviet state, which ceased to belong exclusively to the "proletariat" and became the "all peoples state."

Soviet revisionism never produced a work of much significance. Its main ideas were imported from abroad through the same channels as the Comintern had used to export Soviet propaganda in the 1920s. Andropov's department inherited the Comintern's publishing facilities, together with a small army of translators. The unit functioned under the name of *Progres,* and from the early 1960s one of its tasks became to translate Western social science literature into Russian. These translations were classified, giving the section its name—*Beloy Progres* (*Beloy*/white meant classified).

The selection of literature for translation was made by journalists from *L'Unità* (the paper of the Italian Communist Party), whose Moscow correspondents had the task of advising *Progres* editors. After the Soviet invasion of Czechoslovakia in 1968, the Italian communists withdrew from regular cooperation, and the task of selecting appropriate literature passed to the editors of *The Problems of Peace and Socialism* (*Problemy Mira I Socialisma*), the Soviet journal published in Prague for the "peoples' democracies." This Prague connection enabled some commentators to add the Prague Spring to the intricate intellectual background of perestroika. The Italian communists appear to have been more important than the Czechoslovak dissidents, however; they resumed cooperation inspired by the new idea of introducing more progressive thinking into the Soviet apparatus.

The dissemination of revisionist literature within the Soviet establishment was meticulously organized. Thus, a limited number of copies of *Beloy Progres* in white covers, marked "For internal use only," were distributed within a narrow circle of apparatchiks: Politburo and Central Committee members, the Presidium of the Supreme Soviet, the KGB, the board of the Faculty of Party Schools, and the *obkom* first secretaries. All copies were numbered, and the recipients were obliged to return them by a given date. Frequently, the material was returned straightaway, but there also were requests for prolonged study or for additional literature. Thus, the editors had feedback as to which members of the party apparatus were intellectually curious and open to new ideas. One avid reader was the first secretary of Stavropol province, Mikhail Sergeyevich Gorbachev. In this way he might have first attracted Andropov's attention.[52]

The selection of literature was somewhat predictable. Books about Leon Trotsky and Nikolai Bukharin appeared, together with a slightly less orthodox history of the Soviet Union. Along with a great deal of Italian revisionist literature, other post-Marxist authors were translated, such as Eric Hobsbawm, C. Wright Mills, and John Kenneth Galbraith. From time to time, some Western classics appeared as well, and it was from this source (and certainly not from his law courses at Moscow University, as Remnick had it), that Gorbachev had an opportunity to read John Stuart Mill.

Personnel overlapped between Andropov's intellectuals, the *Progres* editors, and, later on, Gorbachev's ideological team. In that context, Charles Fairbanks put forward the theory of perestroika as a "patrician revolution," that is, an attempt by heirs of the old Bolsheviks "to take back the revolution from the bumpkins who had stolen it."[53] The bumpkins, the theory held, were those whom Stalin put in place of the old Bolshevik elite and who debased the principles of Marxism-Leninism, thus placing the Soviet Union outside the "civilized world." Then came the patricians, that is, Gorbachev's radical advisers, who brought back the high intellectual traditions of the old Bolsheviks and thus made the regime respectable again.

An air of an intellectual rebellion was present during the radical stage of perestroika against the narrow practitioners of the Soviet apparatus of power. But only with some qualifications can these rebels be considered heirs of Lenin's elite. The ideas that Gorbachev's advisers gathered from their flirtation with the Western social sciences were already post-Marxist, not to say postmodernist. Thus, the dogma of class struggle was replaced by theories of globalism and interdependence. Where the iron laws of dialectics once reigned supreme, relativism was slipping in. The theme of unceasing struggle with the capitalist world, backed by massive military buildup, was turned upside-down and construed as a misunderstanding caused by the "lack of proper communication."[54] The West, so recently the implacable enemy, became merely the "enemy's image."[55]

The Poverty of Ideas

Liberated from party discipline, the *Shestidesyatniki* joined the postmodernist wave already sweeping the social sciences in the West. But, unlike their Western counterparts, they were in a position of greater power and joined their ideas with the political agenda of perestroika. Gorbachev and his radical advisers wanted to move beyond the backwaters of Soviet orthodoxy. Social democracy was not anathema to them. In their understanding, socialism had already been achieved in the Soviet Union, and what was left to accomplish was democracy. The Soviet Union was to have a properly elected legislature, and, later on, a popularly elected president, much along American lines.

Neither Gorbachev nor his advisers believed that democracy would make much difference. Elections for the Congress of People's Deputies and republican parliaments, as well as Gorbachev's own election as president, were meant to be mere additions to the existing regime. Jerry Hough already had convinced progressive Soviet apparatchiks that their political system was similar to parliamentary democracy. From C. Wright Mills, they learned that they were as good a "power elite" as the one in the United States. John Kenneth Galbraith showed that capitalist economies and the centrally planned economies were developing in the same direction and would soon become indistinguishable.

Attempts at reform also were encouraged by the revisionist stream in Western Sovietology, which considered the Soviet Union as simply a bad case of bureaucratization, managerial-technocratic takeover, and other assorted ills already diagnosed in Western societies. As for the prospects of maintaining the outer empire under democratic conditions, Gorbachev had it on the highest authority in political science that the difference between colonial and postcolonial dependency would be negligible. The payoff, on the other hand, was seen as considerable: getting rid of the "totalitarian stigma" and placing the Soviet Union on an equal footing with other major powers. From this perspective, democratization and economic reform were not major problems and eventually would take care of themselves (convergency theories). What really mattered for Gorbachev and his elite was to achieve recognition of the Soviet Union as a normal "civilized" (i.e., postcolonial) superpower and to enter the club of Western statesmen.

After studying the written record of ideas that underlined perestroika, one is struck by their intellectual poverty compared to the output from other periods of great reforms, including those from tsarist Russia.[56] It is here that the full depth of the damage done to Russian intellectual life by Stalin's cultural revolution becomes apparent. The Bolsheviks were well-read in the Western canon of philosophy and literature and made ingenious contributions to Marxism. Indeed, their generation proved capable of creative work, even in Stalin's gulags.

Seen in this perspective, the intellectual achievements of Gorbachev's intellectuals are not impressive. Their Aesopian language is sometimes excused by their having been trained in abstract dialectics rather than in reasoning based on facts. But that is not

the point. After all, abstract thinking can be clear and acces-
sible, even if demanding. The documents of perestroika read as if
their authors collected bits and pieces of ideas from various cor-
ners without giving them serious thought. Even the most sympathetic and experienced analysts were at a loss trying to figure
out what it was that the authors of these documents had in mind.
Here is how Archie Brown interpreted Gorbachev's programma-
tic *Pravda* article of November 1989:

Emphasizing that the Soviet Union was part of human civilization, with
a responsibility of conserving it, he went on to say that they had in the
past underestimated the importance of much that had been developed
by humankind over the centuries. He continued: "such achievements of
civilization include not only simple norms of morality and justice, but
also principles of formal law, that is, the equality of all before the law,
individual rights and freedoms, and the principles of commodity production and equivalent exchange based on the operation of the law of
value" (here we have references both to the rule of law and to the market
as part of "civilization," the former advocated unambiguously and the
latter in a more convoluted form. . . .[57] Gorbachev linked the development of socialism with the progress of civilization, arguing: "Democracy
and freedom—these are the great values of human civilization which we
inherit and are filling with socialist content."[58]

Brown duly counted that in this article Gorbachev used the terms
"civilization," "civilized," or derivatives on ten separate occasions,
but he was never fully able to clarify their meaning. Instead,
Brown ventured his own interpretation of the ideas behind perestroika, which in itself remained in the best tradition of a "high"
intellectual discourse:

The acceptance of the possibility of establishing interdependent and
even harmonious relations between "capitalist" and "socialist" systems
went along, naturally enough, with a redefinition of those terms. Both
"socialism" and "capitalism" were concepts which had been employed
to describe a wide variety of political and economic realities, including
"socialist" and "capitalist" *dictatorships,* but in their social democratic
and liberal democratic variants the dividing line between "democratic

socialism" and "democratic capitalism" became quite a fine one. Gorbachev, with his new emphasis on global concerns and universal values, was, in effect, abandoning the idea of a final victory of Communism and legitimizing both a political and economic diversity and an international co-operation which transcended ideological divisions. He was, in a sense, embracing the idea of *convergence of social systems* which had been prematurely, and mainly erroneously, discerned by a number of Western commentators in the Brezhnev era and roundly denounced — also for the wrong reasons — by Soviet ideologists.[59]

It is easy to see how Gorbachev's advisers felt at home in St. Antony's College, Oxford, when invited there to discuss perestroika with Archie Brown, and how little these encounters did to clarify their thinking.

One might argue, however, that this ideological confusion did not greatly matter since the political decisions taken by Gorbachev were much clearer and more consistent, at least as far as foreign policy was concerned. The Soviet leadership's abandonment of the "class approach" in international relations might not have been intellectually impressive, but in practice it meant the end of the cold war. The principle of freedom of choice might have been considered of little consequence if Gorbachev had not announced at the same time the reduction of the Soviet military presence in Eastern Europe, coupled with a commitment to a complete withdrawal of troops in the future. As for domestic reforms, whatever Gorbachev's understanding of democracy may have been, he did introduce contested elections, even though, under the circumstances, they could not have qualified as fully democratic.

The ideas behind perestroika and the New Thinking were clearly secondary to their revealed practice. Nevertheless, as will be shown in chapter 4, the confusion of ideas had serious consequences when it came to handling radical change in international relations caused by the New Thinking. Gorbachev and his advisers seemed to jump from one dogma of "class struggle" to another one of "common human values" without paying much attention to the real world. In this respect it was astounding, yet symptomatic, that neither the Soviet leader, despite being a lawyer by education, nor his closest advisers grasped the importance of the constitutional undertakings leading to German unification.[60] The alternative considered was either art. 146, which would lead to a new constitution, or art. 23, proposing a simple annexation of the GDR, which in fact took place. Apparently, Gorbachev's team shared the postmodernist view that constitutions do not matter. This and other misconceptions on the Soviet side contributed to their gradual loss of leverage over the events triggered by the New Thinking.

Another illustration of the confusion, rooted in the new ideas but overlooked by the Soviet leadership, concerned the Soviet-American dispute over NATO membership of the soon-to-be-united Germany.[61] The ideas floated by the Soviet delegation included membership of a united Germany in both NATO and the Warsaw Pact or the Soviet Union itself joining NATO.[62] After all, what difference would it make in the global and interdependent world? Still another option was a joint declaration by the NATO and Warsaw Pact countries renouncing mutual enmities. This would go against the traditional Soviet doctrine that NATO alone was responsible for the cold war, but it would be consistent with the revised position under the New Thinking, namely, that both sides were equally responsible due to the "lack of communication."

However, such a presumption of moral equivalence between NATO and the Warsaw Pact was not much to Kohl's liking, and Gorbachev had to make do with NATO's unilateral declaration that the Soviet Union was no longer its enemy. One may admire Kohl's nerve in taking such a principled stance at the moment when the fate of his country was in the balance. At the same time, however, it is difficult to understand why Gorbachev gave up a point that would have secured an important moral victory for the Soviet Union. He seemed to have scant understanding of the difference at the time.

The utopia of nonpolitical international relations based on theories of globalism and interdependence that pervaded the New

Thinking left little room for considerations of national interest or, as Eduard Shevardnadze's memoirs make abundantly clear, for any strategic thinking at all.[63] In this way post-Marxist ideas came to play their part in the dismantling of the Marxist regime. One may ponder the political potential of a theory that had first armed a superpower and subsequently paralyzed it by severing its ideological stem.

The Man and the Regime

Gorbachev proved time and again his skills in political maneuvering between various factions within the party, and he knew well how to get support from people whose help he needed. But when it came to the day-to-day business of government, let alone radical reform, his managerial skills appeared to be poor, an opinion shared by friends and foes alike. Part of the problem might have been the very nature of Soviet institutions, which, as will be argued in chapter 2, were poorly structured and at the mercy of powerful personalities. Nevertheless, a closer look into the ways in which Gorbachev and his radical advisers handled the institutional side of their reforms makes one wonder about their practical sense of administration.

The dismantling of the only functioning administrative machinery, whatever its nature, without preparing another to replace it, was careless, to say the least. Yet this was what Gorbachev did when he undercut the executive powers of the Central Committee Secretariat in 1988. The gap left behind by the emasculated CC Secretariat was to be filled by the Presidential Council. The general idea was to shift powers from the party into "the hands of a legitimate state authority."[64] But the idea itself could not replace the existing operational structures that were being abandoned. The Presidential Council, in turn, was nothing more than the president (i.e., Gorbachev) and a group of his most trusted advisers. No institutional structure sufficiently underpinned the Presidential Council to make it an effective executive: "What he ended up with was a multi-layer confusion, with the Presidential Council, and above that the Federation Council, and above that, in theory at least, the executive power of the government, all of them constantly consulting and advising but none capable of taking a decision."[65]

In the end, it was the best in Gorbachev as a person that made him ultimately lose power together with his empire. His most important decisions were those that he did not take or that he hesitated too long before taking. Whatever his part in the violent episodes under his rule, such as the assault on the Baltic capitals in January 1991, or even in the August putsch, taking coercive measures went against his basic instincts. He inherited a despotic regime in a state of decline, and while trying to enlighten it he rescinded the only effective instrument that he had left—its armed forces. Various reasons can be put forward for Gorbachev's unwillingness to use the army as a political instrument (to be discussed in chapter 3). But few can doubt that he was a man of peace, that he dreaded bloodshed. Happily married, he knew how to enjoy life. Such men are not made to run despotic regimes, let alone to reform them.

Chapter 2

Horizontal Disintegration:
The Center-Periphery Conflict

Every house, village, not to mention every town and province, had its little tyrant (at first there would be several, until a single one took over), who gave orders and instructions, threatening always to "make mince-meat" of anyone who resisted. . . . Everywhere there were blustering bullies carrying on like this. —Nadezhda Mandelstam, on the first years of Lenin's rule[1]

At the time when Mikhail Gorbachev assumed the highest post in the Soviet Union, the powers of the center already had been severely reduced. The military-industrial sector, as well as some long-standing republican leaders, had practically gone unchallenged for about two decades. The surge of baronial power in the Soviet Union resembled what historians called "bastard feudalism," power relations similar to those that spread in Europe after the Hundred Years War.[2]

A peculiar feature of bastard feudalism was that, although factional struggles destroyed authority, no enduring institutions were created as a result: "power shifts rapidly from one factional leader to another," and the purpose of the political game is "not to create a new government, but rather to get control of some part of the existing one." Similarly, in the fragmented post-Stalinist regime, although factional struggles strongly undermined central government, those conflicts had never gone so far as to destroy the existing political system. This system had to be preserved to generate further opportunities for the ruling elite.

As the newly elected general secretary, Gorbachev's choice was either to preside over further emasculation of his office, which was the Brezhnev way, or to attempt the reconstruction of central authority. Perestroika meant the route of reconstruction. Gorbachev's main objective was not to decentralize an omnipotent state, as many analysts suggested, for no such thing existed in the Soviet Union at that time. On the contrary, his task was to concentrate powers that had dissipated from the Soviet center during the Brezhnev years. Thus, perestroika can be better understood as a state-building enterprise, rather than an attempt to curb the state, its design being determined by the frailty of the Soviet center rather than by its strength.

The Logic of Perestroika

Major reforms were directed onto two fronts. The first was a classical center-periphery struggle. Owing to the weakness of the administrative institutions and the sheer size of the country, Soviet power had to be delegated to local enforcers on a more or less generalist principle. This principle inadvertently led to central powers being appropriated by territorial leaders. In fact, long before grassroots popular fronts emerged in the Soviet republics, the party apparatus had been divided into regional factions. Although officials at the center could make and break single apparatchiks, they found it increasingly difficult to control a consolidated local elite.

In a multinational empire, ethnicity is the most obvious source of center-periphery friction. In fact, the ethnic factor in local consolidation could not be doubted, especially in the Asian republics. But similar developments were recorded in the Russian territories as well. For example, the cities of Leningrad and Moscow were the fiefdoms of their long-standing party leaders, Grigory Romanov and Victor Grishin, respectively.[3] The aim of perestroika was to break these fiefdoms and to make them more amenable to central steering, or, in other words, to centralize the fragmented regime.

The second conflict arose along a vertical axis, involving the

only two Soviet institutions of a strong Union identity, as opposed
to a regional one. These were the KGB and the army. A balance
between the KGB and the military was maintained by subjecting
them equally to political control by the party. The precondition
for the party to exercise such control, however, was that it maintained the cohesion of its own apparatus. Toward the mid-1970s
the party apparatus not only lost its capacity to supervise the
forces of coercion, but it became involved on both sides of their
conflict. With a diminishing degree of supervision and arbitration above them, it was only a question of time before these two
pillars of the regime confronted each other in a lethal contest.

The military-KGB rivalry reached its peak at the end of the
seventies when the succession to the terminally sick Brezhnev
was to be decided. The accession of Yuri Andropov in 1982 meant
that the KGB gained the upper hand, which was confirmed by the
series of antimilitary policies that he pursued during the short
period of his rule. Gorbachev inherited the KGB-military feud
from his late patron together with his mantle.

The two axes of conflict, horizontal-territorial and vertical-
institutional, will be discussed in coming chapters. Now, my in-
tent is to show that fragmentation of the Soviet Union, both
territorial and institutional, had deep structural causes associated
with the arbitrary nature of the regime.

Managing Soviet Nationalities

The stir of national sentiments accelerated the disintegration of
the Soviet Union and has remained among the most visible problems on the former Union's territory. Has the rise of nationalisms, however, been an ever-present threat to the Soviet regime?
I shall argue that this was not the case and that the explosion of
nationalisms in the Soviet Union was as much activated by the
breakdown of central structures as it contributed, in its turn, to
the regime's final demolition.

The first part of my argument concerns the traditional Soviet policy on nationalities, which had proved fairly effective in neutralizing the potential for national uprisings. It was the change of this policy, initiated by Andropov and pursued further by Gorbachev, that first provoked ethnic unrest. The reasons for this change are the subject of a separate debate. In the second part of my argument, I consider the deep structural causes of the territorial fragmentation of the Soviet regime. My purpose is to show that these causes were at least as much systemic in origin as they were contingent on the ethnic factor.

The Soviet Union had managed to muddle through several crises, most notably World War II and the first post-Stalinist decade, without serious threat of national rebellions. It also had managed to effectively neutralize the vigorous nationalisms of formerly independent peoples, such as the Balts, Poles, or Hungarians. Up to Gorbachev's time, Soviet policy on nationalities was, next to foreign policy, an area of considerable success, at least as far as the interests of the center were concerned.[4]

Coercion undoubtedly played its part, but only up to a point. Such measures as shuttling entire populations across the continent could be performed only by force. This contributed to uprooting many peoples and sowing discord among others. In the post-Stalinist period, however, coercion receded, remaining an ever-present threat but not the sole measure in managing the Soviet nationalities. Soviet leaders applied a number of policies to separate national elites from their ethnic bases and to manage ethnic conflicts to the leadership's benefit.

The solutions adopted were simple and effective. Nationalities were ordered into a territorial hierarchy (union republics, autonomous republics, autonomous provinces and districts) with the titular nationality given the upper hand in its territory over non-titulars, including Russians. When two titulars clashed, assistance was given to the group deemed capable of making more trouble, as was the case with the Azeris in their conflict with the Armenians.

The borders were drawn in a way that ensured permanent conflicts between neighboring ethnic groups, thus rendering unlikely their collusion against the center. A classical case in point was the creation of the new Soviet republic of Moldova out of the territory annexed by Stalin from Romania and the Trans-Dniestrian strip carved from Ukraine. The present government of Moldova has been just as unwilling to give up the Ukrainian part of its territory as it is incapable of integrating the Ukrainian minority with the Romanian section of society.

Perhaps the most effective policies on Soviet nationalities were the measures aimed at separating national elites from their ethnic bases. To this purpose, an almost impermeable wall was erected between the cities and the countryside (known as the policy of closed cities), and internal passports were required for the villagers.[5] These policies prevented the well-known scenario that had given rise to modern nationalism: a country youth coming to the metropolis to study and returning to his native stock with modern ideas. In that way the Lithuanian peasants had the opportunity of learning nationalism from their native intelligentsia educated at the Polish university in Vilnius. No such diffusion of ideas was possible between the university of Alma-Ata and the collective farms in Kazakhstan.

In Ukraine, where the status of white-collar workers was conferred almost by birth and most blue-collar workers were descended from Russian immigrants, there was little chance that industrial unrest could be combined with the National Front in the struggle for national independence. Rigid social, ethnic, and geographic barriers prevented collusion among classes, which arrested the development of effective national movements. If ethnic grievances occurred, they only strengthened the role of the Soviet center, as has been the case with the Georgian-Ossetian conflict.

Before Gorbachev, the Soviet leadership used to be on guard on the question of nationalities. This was evident in the central personnel policy for non-Russian republican parties and state administrations, where the native intelligentsia held priority in their titular republics. Each union republic had the entire set of standard Soviet institutions, beginning with the party and government structures and extending to the replication of all other central organizations such as youth and trade unions, the Academy of Sciences, etc. Thus, jobs were plentiful, and the republican elites were well integrated into the Soviet regime, having their personal stakes deeply invested in it. Generally, the Soviet policy on nationalities was successful, and it took more than just an ailing center for the impulse toward national liberation to be activated in earnest.

The Central-Local Rift

The key to stability was found in maintaining a balance between the interests of the central elite and its republican counterparts. Brezhnev cultivated the interests of peripheral leaders, and he maintained excellent (if corrupt) relations with all the republican mafiosi. For example, he would never have dreamed of arbitrarily firing the long-standing Kazakh leader, Dinmukhamed Kunayev, and replacing him with a Russian, as Gorbachev did in 1986, thus provoking his first nationality problem.

The repeal of traditional privileges of republican elites was initiated by Andropov when, as head of the KGB, he launched a series of anticorruption campaigns. Andropov's motives in starting these efforts were disputed at the time. According to Michael Voslensky, by making the case against corruption, Andropov was able to employ his institution's resources in the struggle to succeed the aging Brezhnev. Thousands of convictions were meted out in local anticorruption campaigns, which were, according to Voslensky, just rehearsals for the main spectacle prepared in Moscow.[6] When the time of succession came, Andropov was able to intimidate the entire Politburo into voting for him.

In fact, anticorruption campaigns ceased as soon as Andropov became the top leader since he well understood the limits of the regime over which he presided. The same campaigns were resuscitated by Gorbachev under the banner of glasnost. His first target was the Kazakh leadership, but the riots in Alma-Ata made him more careful. Nevertheless, Gorbachev did not back off, carry-

ing out wholesale purges in republican administrations and re-
placing entire local elites by means of arbitrary central decisions.
Such things had been unthinkable during the last two decades of
Brezhnev rule.

Zaslavsky has explained this rapid change in traditional Soviet
personnel policies by economic concerns.[7] True, the cultivation of
local elites in the Union republics required the maintenance of expensive, oversized administrations. Nevertheless, disturbing the
balance between the center and the republics proved still more
expensive, in both economic and political terms. Some researchers have shown that a more conservative Soviet leadership would
have had reasonable room for maneuver in the economy without
exposing the regime's foundations.[8]

Central Planning and Territorial Fragmentation

The Soviet economy was doubtless much less effective than the
market economies of the West, but in the 1980s it was showing
no signs of immediate collapse. The fallacy of purely economic
explanations of perestroika has been demonstrated in analyses
showing that Gorbachev actually overstated the dire straits of the
Soviet economy in his first appeals, probably to make a better case
for his radical policies.[9]

In the command economy the root cause of stagnation is usually
the command system itself. As in a war economy when money is
not an objective, the system can work only when based on a few
key priorities.[10] In the period of rapid industrialization, economic
priorities were maintained by means of terror. As soon as the terror subsided, communist leaders were confronted with demands
that their government was ill-equipped to satisfy. The range of
priorities broadened to account for several neglected areas, such
as housing and consumer goods, and, as a result, the economy
defied any system of central control. Consequently, certain economic responsibilities devolved to the provinces.

At the end of the 1950s about 80 percent of the national economies in the Soviet bloc were managed by specially constituted regional economic councils.[11] In the Soviet Union the area of their jurisdiction did not coincide with the country's administrative divisions. Therefore, one may guess that the regional party committees were not supposed to control the economic resources located in their regions.[12] In the absence of markets, however, economic enterprises depended a great deal on political backing, and the only sources of effective political authority below the center were the territorial party committees. Thus, the industrial managerial elite became effectively incorporated into the local power structures.

The cohesion of republican elites was credited to the ethnic factor. To be sure, ethnicity was helpful in consolidating a local elite, but this was by no means the single, still less the decisive, factor. In the Russian Republic itself, overt demands for devolution of economic responsibilities to regional (*obkom*) party committees were recorded as early as the mid-1970s.[13] Specifically, the *obkom* secretaries demanded that competencies for planning and supply should be firmly established at the regional level; the role of *obkom* party committees in deciding regional priorities should increase; a single coordinating center for the regional economy should be set up in each *obkom*, with authority to override directives coming from central departments.

The regional apparatchiks of the Brezhnev era were hardly revisionists; they did not demand any radical change in the status quo but merely an official recognition and expansion of what had already been a widespread practice.

Patrimonial Regression

The merger of economic and political power in the republics and *obkoms* had two important consequences. First, republican and regional party leaders acquired broad access to material resources on which to build their own patronage networks. Second, as economic resources diminished, the bargaining position of those able to control them increased. A bargain struck between the center and territorial party leaders transformed the territorial apparatchiks into a "semiaristocratic" group. According to S. N. Eisenstadt, such regression to patrimonial, particularistic officeholdings was a cyclical characteristic of prebureaucratic regimes.[14]

At the fragmented stage of the planned economy, territorial party leaders resembled tributary lords, fighting for the highest possible investments and the lowest production targets for their regions. The concealment of resources by middle-level and lower-level officials used to be interpreted in terms of corruption. This phenomenon was indeed widespread, one that weighed heavily on the national economy. Material gain in itself, however, need not be the only reason why regional leaders divert resources from their centrally planned destination. In a system where access to goods (whether raw materials for a local factory or foodstuffs for a local shop) depends almost exclusively on authoritative allocation, the ability to deliver them determines one's position in a very primordial sense. The phenomenon corresponds to G. M. Foster's notion of the "image of limited good" typical of peasant societies.[15]

In certain circumstances a local party leader was able to acquire the status of political authority in his own right, first, because he was capable of undertaking the authoritative allocation of scarce resources, and second, because he alone had the right to mediate with the center. Various countermeasures were undertaken by the center to prevent the excessive growth of local personality cults. For example, the Central Committee Secretariat was sensitive on the issue of regional party leaders having their pictures displayed in the local press.[16] Other than that, however, the supervision of regional party committees was superficial.

Between Center and Periphery:
The Pendulum of Soviet Reforms

Attempts at economic recentralization were initiated across the entire bloc by Kosygin reforms in the mid-1960s and led to the regrouping of particular sectors of industry into "combines." These were multifactory conglomerates, integrated to cross-cut the jurisdictions of territorial party committees. The boards of the combines were directly subject to the central ministries, and their formal channels of command bypassed territorial party authorities. The main objective was to confine industrial management within the structures of the economic administration and to prevent lateral interference from the territorial party apparatus.

The center's attempts to reclaim control over the most valuable areas of the national economy were vigorously resisted by the territorial party apparatuses in all communist countries. The struggle between departmental and territorial authorities proceeded under two slogans: the "production principle" represented the interests of the center, whereas the "principle of coordination" was to defend regional prerogatives. Both principles crop up repeatedly in party debates throughout the Soviet bloc in the mid-sixties.

As a rule, the weaker the position of a particular industrial sector in the center, the more its resources were exposed to the local "principle of coordination." For example, cotton production was particularly vulnerable to local control by regional party bosses, for the ministries responsible for agriculture and the textile industry had little political clout at the center. As a result, large amounts of cotton were diverted to black markets.[17] In contrast, heavy industry, especially that part connected to the military, was much more autonomous. Regional secretaries knew only too well that interfering with military plants operating in their territories was politically unsafe.[18]

Kosygin's reforms were largely unsuccessful, as the demotion of their author shows. Brezhnev's ascendancy meant in practice that the "principle of coordination" was vindicated. As a result, only the East German combines survived until the end of the regime to give headaches to those responsible for the post-communist transition. In the Soviet Union, although the interests of the military-industrial sector were safely secured, the strongest republics managed to keep many of their economic resources under their own control. As Alec Nove has pointed out, the inherent impossibility of effective centralization caused most of the problems faced by the Soviet economy in the 1970s.[19] Nove described the symptoms of economic fragmentation, but he failed to explain the prime mechanisms inherent in the very practice of Soviet central planning.

The Chicken and Egg Dilemma

Beginning in the early 1950s a general relaxation within the command structure resulted in a persistent slowdown in the Soviet economy.[20] This trend was noticed by Western economists only in the late sixties; nevertheless, those concerned with forecasting "the future performance of the Soviet economy seemed oblivious to the possibility that the trend would continue."[21]

Andropov addressed the problem by tightening the discipline of the administrative apparatus, meaning that some ministers were replaced and the failures of others were increasingly sanctioned. "This simple strategy . . . caused growth to rebound in a matter of months and provided the momentum that carried the Soviet economy through the 1980s."[22] Similar tactics were applied by Gorbachev in the antialcohol campaign and in a massive shift of investments into sectors deemed more profitable. The results of these policies never had a chance to materialize because the entire strategy of Gorbachev's reforms changed radically, beginning in the second half of 1987.

The major difficulty in reforming this kind of regime is the necessity to change the political and economic structures simultaneously. The imposition of the rule of law, providing it is possible, may instantly paralyze the mobilization of economic resources. On the other hand, no market mechanisms can operate under a system of arbitrary rule. All communist reformers were confronted with this chicken-and-egg dilemma. No evidence indicates, however, that Gorbachev was fully aware of it when he started his battle with Soviet local "notables."

The Bloodless Purge

The scale and pace of personnel changes in the party apparatus in the second half of the 1980s was unprecedented in Soviet history. Four years into his leadership, Gorbachev had replaced more than four-fifths of the top party leaders. Newcomers filled more than nine-tenths of the higher government positions and three-quarters of the leading posts in the republics and regions.[23] This changeover came on top of substantial replacements already made by his predecessors Yuri Andropov and Konstantin Chernenko. The rapid turnover was justified in part by the aging of Brezhnev's generation. However, changes in the territorial party apparatus went far beyond the usual turnover under new leadership and even beyond the change of generations in power.

Gorbachev did not stop with one-off replacements, but he kept changing his own appointees at a rate comparable to that of the Stalinist purges.[24] Stalinist policies also were resuscitated in onslaughts in the press against territorial party apparatuses. "This was a vintage communist campaign: high pitch, unrelenting, blanket demagogy" against local officials and "bureaucrats,"[25] Vladimir Kantorovich wrote. Although the most important part of the Great Purges—the terror—was missing, the destruction of local and regional party centers was occurring much the same at the end of the eighties as it had at the end of the thirties.[26]

Deep incursions into central party structures were decided on at the CC Plenum in August 1988. The once powerful Central Committee Secretariat, that is, the de facto Soviet government for the preceding quarter-century, was turned into a talking shop. The full-time staff of the Secretariat was cut by 30 percent, and the status of its departments changed from permanent working organs into occasionally assembling commissions. The Politburo started to meet irregularly, once a month or so, and then only to consider party matters.[27]

To a large extent, the economic breakdown that ensued was the result of the destruction of political authority and administration at the local level, caused by the relentless personnel policy.

As authority weakened, more political players were drawn into the game
. . . . Instead of making the system more flexible and dynamic, each
newly organized group tore into its fabric. In the late 1980s, the economy was hurt by ethnic hostilities, miners' strikes, and strike threats in
other sectors, shutdowns of chemical and power plants by environmental protesters, and the assertion of sovereignty by local governments . . .
the East European revolutions disrupted trade within the CMEA, delivering another blow to the already reeling system.[28]

From Terror to Patronage;
The Paradoxes of Arbitrary Rule

The key systemic cause of the territorial fragmentation of the
Soviet Union was the arbitrary nature of the Soviet regime. Historical research has shown how arbitrary governments succumb to
centrifugal forces inherent in their own apparatuses of power;[29]
the arbitrary manner of decision making at the center is replicated at all levels of the hierarchy, consequently undermining the
center's own discretion.

Lenin first discovered that the Soviet state was "like a car that
was not going in the direction the driver desired, but in the direction someone else desired; as if it was driven by some mysterious
lawless hand, God knows whose. . . ."[30] Unlimited dictatorial
powers transformed revolutionaries into "veritable feudal lords"
who took personal offense at any attempts at supervision from
above. Right from the beginning of the Soviet regime, regional
secretaries cut autocratic figures, having factories and districts
named after them. Lenin demanded that corrupt communists be
"tried on the spot and shot, unconditionally."[31] But at the time,
that was easier said than done.

It took a bloodbath of party officials in the Great Purge to
make them toe the party line. The interpretation of the Great
Purge as a conclusion to central-local rivalry for power has been
well-documented by J. A. Getty.[32] Although Getty tried to sub-
stantiate a preposterous thesis that Stalinist society was pluralist,
and he saw the signs of "vigorous debates" in the Stalinist press

campaigns, his findings from the period of the Great Purge tell their own story. They highlight an important and much neglected aspect of the Soviet government—that is, the difficulty of consolidating arbitrary rule.

In the post-Stalinist era the regime's stability was based on a balance of interests between the central and peripheral elites. At this stage, regional party leaders had entrenched themselves in their local fiefdoms and turned into notables with power resources of their own. Revolutionary vigilance gave way to corruption as the principal mechanism of the regime's consolidation. The fusion of private and public criteria, or the "privatization of the state,"[33] was a natural consequence of revolutionary terror from the previous stage. Both terror and corruption were equally lawless manifestations of arbitrary rule.

A similar shift of central-local relations from terror to patronage appears as a general rule in the history of all communist regimes. In each case we can find the unimposing figure of a CC secretary; he is the one responsible for "organizational matters," who quietly engages in empire-building by means of carefully selected appointments to regional party posts. When the time of succession comes, our modest secretary has already secured his power base in the territorial apparatus, and with the help of his clients he usually gains the upper hand over more prominent runners.

Such were the roots of the victory of Stalin over Trotsky, Khrushchev over the "antiparty group," and Brezhnev over Kosygin. Andropov was apparently an exception, since he had held the key post of secretary for organization in the CC for only a few months before he became general secretary. That was too short a time to build support in the provincial apparatuses. Nevertheless (as explained in more detail in chapter 3), Andropov had set up his own network of loyal regional and republican secretaries as chair of the KGB.

By the late 1960s, regional party leaders in several communist countries had acquired a say in the sensitive matter of leadership succession. Having won over the "antiparty" group at the center,

Khrushchev fell victim to his own territorial apparatus as soon as he tried to curb their newly acquired powers by imposing the rule of rotation. "The apparatchiks had submitted to Stalin's rotation-through-terror," but rotation "according to law was more than they could stomach."[34] After Khrushchev's removal, the rotation rule was immediately renounced. The same scenario developed in other communist countries, regardless of their ethnic composition, which shows that the phenomenon was systemic.

Regional party leaders became involved in the succession struggles in Romania, Poland, and East Germany. While holding the post of CC secretary of organization, Nicolae Ceauşescu managed to build a coalition with regional first secretaries. On his accession to power in 1965, he promoted eleven of them to leading posts in the Romanian party and state hierarchy.[35] The first promotions to the German Politburo following Erich Honecker's takeover in 1971 were provincial (*Bezirk*) party leaders, who were his "favorite clientele."[36] In Poland the leadership of the strongest province (Silesia) brought Edvard Gierek to the highest post in 1970. In Czechoslovakia the new federal constitution of 1968, which meant a de facto administrative autonomy for the Slovak party apparatus, was the only reform of the Prague Spring that survived the period of "normalization." It gave the Slovak communists a degree of autonomy from Prague that they had never enjoyed before.

The paramount role of the regional party leaders was reflected in the Soviet Union as well as in other communist countries in their growing membership in the Central Committee and also in their ever-increasing terms of office.[37] At the peak of their powers, the regional secretaries were in almost complete charge of appointments to the most important positions located in their territory and were themselves either natives or long-term residents in their regions.[38] In this way the regional party apparatchiks became transformed from disposable agents of the center into local notables, with an increasing power base of their own.

Gorbachev's "Third Way"

Although the issue of reconstructing central authority had entered the Soviet leadership's agenda only on Gorbachev's accession, two other communist leaders, Ceauşescu in Romania and Gierek in Poland, had carried out their own perestroikas in the seventies. At that time, Poland and Romania underwent radical restructuring of their territorial administrations, leading to the dispersing of local patronage networks and the strengthening of vertical channels of command.[39] Similar attempts were made in East Germany and Bulgaria to remove the administration of industry and agriculture from the hands of the territorial party apparatuses.

In retrospect, it is easy to understand why attempts at reconstruction began at the periphery of the Soviet empire rather than at its center. Certainly the scale of difficulties faced by Gorbachev was far greater than anything that Ceauşescu or Gierek had ever encountered. Nevertheless, some common features can be identified in all attempts at reforming a post-Stalinist regime.

Reformers faced a major dilemma: How to concentrate their fragmented powers without resorting to terror? The solution was usually a peaceful version of "revolution from above," shifting the power base from the party to the state. In the process, leadership needed popular support to neutralize incumbent local and regional party elites. In Poland a kind of "social contract" was achieved by raising the standard of living. This tactic soon proved incompatible with economic capacity, and in 1980–81 the solution by force was left as the only way for the regime to survive social unrest. In Romania, Ceauşescu's emphasis on national independence helped him enlist public support. For a while he considered a "Polish option" of increasing living standards, but he turned to Stalinist tactics in the end. Open terror secured his power for the next twenty years.

Gorbachev's glasnost and democratization—instead of either material improvement or terror—may be considered a "third way" of winning popular support in the process of reconstruction. Victoria Bonnel reached a similar conclusion when she wrote: "Like Stalin, Gorbachev needs mass mobilization to carry out a vast restructuring of economic, social and political institutions."[40]

A Police-Sponsored Revolution

Informal organizations often were not only encouraged but initiated on instructions from above.[41] This was a scientific project of social change, coordinated by Soviet sociologists and, in many cases, sponsored by the KGB. The traces of this institution have been discovered in the origins of several popular front organizations, such as Birlik in Azerbaijan[42] and Sajudis in Lithuania.[43] This initiative, of course, could not possibly stop the emergence of truly independent social and national movements that soon escaped engineering from the center.

The extraordinary idea of a police-sponsored civil society was not entirely new. It reflected the age-old illusion of dictators — that it is possible to experiment with democracy while keeping a cap ready in case it works against the reformers themselves. In the Soviet Union such an illusion was reinforced by the deep-rooted belief of the security services in their ability to engineer and direct social movements. The origins of this confidence reached back to Lenin's concept of professional revolutionaries as the only force capable of raising and directing a mass movement. Lenin's conception was, in turn, a response to the tsarist security device of police-sponsored "revolutionary cells." Both traditions were revived with perestroika; at that time, just as at the end of the tsarist regime, it was difficult to tell a rebel from a police agent.

The tsarist police were incapable of containing genuine social unrest when it occurred in Russia. That is, they would have been able to do so, had it been the professional revolutionaries who made Russian revolutions, for their network was deeply penetrated by the police. All of the agents implanted in the revolutionary cells proved useless, however, since Lenin's professional revolutionaries had little to do with igniting the two genuine Russian revolutions, in 1905 and 1917, though they managed to hijack the second one.[44] Perestroika worked the other way round. Once in power, the heirs of the professional revolutionaries succeeded in igniting a revolution, but they failed to keep it under control.

When power elites are in conflict, the public becomes an increasingly independent actor. This is how democracy takes off and the political process escapes the total control of any single actor. The national fronts, their artificial origins notwithstanding, soon adopted the most obvious local and national agenda, ranging from various measures of autonomy to complete secession, depending on place and time. From then on, the two-corner game between the central and republican party leaders turned into a three-corner one, with the republican "counter-elite" emerging as an independent actor. Such a three-corner game could have proved viable to continue for a considerable time if only the center had held. The center was badly split, however, by the emergence of the Russian government parallel, and soon the alternative, to the Soviet one.

The Soviet-Russian conflict, which became the decisive factor of disintegration, cannot be explained in purely national terms. The multiethnicity of the Russian Federation was of little significance in the inception of this lethal split. In fact, the Russians failed to form a national front of their own for lack of an agreement over what "Russian" should mean.[45] The Russian parliament was dominated by disgruntled apparatchiks, who suffered from Gorbachev's perestroika as much as, or even more, than party notables from other republics. Having waged war on the Soviet center by the declaration of sovereignty in June 1990, the Russian parliament was bound to become a leaderless and unmangeable body. Yeltsin just managed to get elected as its chairman, but he had to search for a power base and legitimacy in a popular election.

Stalin's and Gorbachev's "Revolutions from Above": The Soviet Cycle

Why Gorbachev set out to destroy his own apparatus of power has remained largely unexplained. According to a popular interpretation, he had grown disappointed with the abilities of the party apparatus to deliver what he wanted, even after massive personnel changes took place. Simply not enough talented people devoted to change held positions within the nomenklatura system, Gorbachev said. The pool available for selection was to be extended by democratic means, but it soon became obvious that such measures mostly served to oust those deemed unfit for office while replacing them with others sent directly from Moscow.

The only other Soviet leader who performed a similar "revolution from above" was Stalin. To see a parallel between Gorbachev's and Stalin's policies at first may seem startling. After all, Gorbachev presided over the genuine de-Stalinization of the Soviet Union, no matter how much he disliked the consequences of that effort. Moreover, it would be difficult to find two men more different in their disposition toward applying violent means; Gorbachev could hardly stomach violence, whereas for Stalin violence was a reflex response to immediate political and economic problems. Another significant difference between the two leaders regards their attitude toward the outside world. If Stalin tried to fence off his empire from external influence, Gorbachev's objective was to integrate the USSR and its satellites into the modern system of international relations.

More relevant than those differences, however, is the cyclical character of the Soviet regime, which originated in the massive application of terror and never developed more reliable instruments of maintaining centralized power. At the beginnings of their rule, both Stalin and Gorbachev found themselves at the same point of the Soviet cycle when the entrenchment of the party apparatus in the provinces spells the end to effective centralization.

Gorbachev's and Stalin's "antibureaucratic" campaigns had a similar purpose: the reconstruction of central power. Although the means they employed could not have been more different, their notions of power seemed similar, and these notions meant their freedom from whatever constraints might limit their personal discretion. Very much like Stalin, Gorbachev treated the business of government as his personal affair, and both leaders lacked either the necessary understanding or the patience to create lasting institutions. As a result, both men managed to destroy whatever institutional settings they found at the start of their rule, but neither of them left behind much in the way of a stable regime.

Such governing bodies created by Gorbachev as the Presidential Council, the Presidential Cabinet, or the Chamber of Federation had few executive capacities (see chapter 1). After the dispossession of the Central Committee Secretariat, which had been the real Soviet government since the early sixties, the only remaining central institution that had some executive powers was the Council of Ministers. In fact, toward the end of the 1980s the Council of Ministers was practically the only all-Union institution left with powers extending to the republican governments. To tinker with the Council of Ministers at that time meant exposing the precarious links between Moscow and the republics, a dangerous undertaking when links within the party apparatus already had been severely weakened.

Anatoly Lukyanov, the experienced operator of the Congress of People's Deputies, advised Gorbachev to leave the Council of Ministers alone since it was vital for the new legislature to function. Lukyanov operated the Congress of People's Deputies through applying cross-cutting departmental pressures to circumvent republican coteries. This balance was upset when Gorbachev disbanded the Council of Ministers, which was the mainstay of departmental interests, and replaced it with the Presidential Cabinet—a weakly structured body consisting of his personal advisers. Lukyanov predicted that, as a result, the cleavage between Moscow and the republics would become even more difficult to manage, and the Congress of People's Deputies would break up. In fact, this happened in the spring of 1991 when the republics opened a separate makeshift legislature—the Soviet version of the roundtable in Novo-Ogarovo:

> I told him that in three months after the Congress breaks up, you will also cease to be President. . . . I knew on what basis the opposition was working. I participated in Novo-Ogarovo talks . . . Brezhnev or Andropov had understood that without the support of the party, they were nobody . . . [but Gorbachev] . . . was deluded by the idea that the country and the people needed him as an individual. He did not take account of the fact that if he abandoned the party and socialism and loyal comrades, then he would ultimately find himself superfluous.[46]

In a way, Gorbachev's reforms followed the logic of the despotic regime he tried to reform. Like Lenin, and Stalin later, he eradicated the existing structures because they set limits to his grand projects. But in such a deinstitutionalized environment, no leadership could have been sustained except by means of terror.

The Winding Up of Perestroika

Was the return to terror a realistic option for Gorbachev? It was not included in the initial scenario of perestroika. Nevertheless, as the turmoil spread, voices were heard in favor of the return of Stalinism; such were the demands of the conservative apparatus, represented by Nina Andreyeva in an open letter published in March 1988 in the Soviet press.[47] The same section of the Soviet apparatus was back at the wheel by the autumn of 1990, reinstated by Gorbachev as the only reliable power base from which to confront Boris Yeltsin. At this stage the use of terror became a question of technical capacity rather than choice; regardless of Gorbachev's real role in the 1991 August coup, his personnel policy during the preceding year paved the way to this outcome. (The causes of his failure to actually deliver a forcible solution will be discussed in chapter 3.)

The emergence of the incipient Russian government, headed by Yeltsin, in the spring of 1990 left Gorbachev with little choice but to turn to the party and its apparatus for support. This he did at the Twenty-Eighth (and last) Party Congress in July 1990. At this session, Gorbachev had to answer for the undermining of party structures and the creation of social, political, and economic upheaval throughout the country, not to mention the loss of control over East Central Europe. Hardly anyone expected him to get away with all these setbacks, and his reelection as general secretary seemed problematic. The inner-party opposition to Gorbachev already had a leader in Yegor Ligachev.

Once again, Gorbachev showed his brilliance as a tactician in party skirmishes. He offered the aggrieved apparatchiks far-reaching concessions. First of all, each republican party leader received a voting seat in the Politburo. Since the republican parties preserved their "democratic centralism" (meaning, they were able to control the votes of republican representatives) much better than the All-Union CP, placating the republican leaders won Gorbachev the votes of the non-Russian republics. The Russian section of the Congress was in disarray, and Gorbachev could count on at least some part of its votes. The hard line was represented by the newly formed Russian Communist Party,[48] whereas the liberals behind Yeltsin walked out of the Congress. Yeltsin's walkout strengthened Gorbachev's hand by putting him in the center and offering a common enemy to all Russians who stayed on.

At this Congress, Gorbachev changed the procedure for electing the general secretary. Instead of the usual Central Committee vote, both the general secretary and his deputy were to be elected by the entire Congress. This was a shrewd maneuver, since Ligachev's supporters were relatively more influential in the Central Committee than in the Congress at large. In the end, Gorbachev was reelected by the entire Congress, which also strengthened his position in the party. His main opponent, Ligachev, failed to get the position of second secretary, to which the Ukrainian first secretary, Vladimir Ivashko, was elected. Thus, the matter was settled on the basis of territorial representation.

Gorbachev's victory at the Twenty-Eighth Congress won him the appraisal of commentators, who nevertheless missed its peculiar significance. The new composition of the Politburo made the All-Union Party structures de facto federal; each republic acquired equal representation in the highest decision-making body, with the two largest republics (Russia and Ukraine) at the leading posts. Thus, Gorbachev's victory at the Congress also marked his failure to achieve the original objective of perestroika, which was recentralization of the fragmented Soviet regime. In other words, the Soviet center gave up its centralistic claims, and the composition of the Politburo was adjusted to accommodate the demands of the peripheries.

The question, however, was how much of a regime was left to secure a safe return to the status quo ante after five years of perestroika and glasnost. National fronts and other civic and political organizations already had either dominated republican parliaments or formed strong opposition groups within them. The press was flooded with criticisms of the party, which sometimes was called a criminal organization. Last but not least, developments in East Central Europe, where communist parties, reformed or not, lost the first democratic elections, were having an impact on some Soviet republics (especially in the Baltics and Caucasus). In such circumstances a peaceful restoration of the traditional Soviet regime was out of the question.

Gorbachev duly adopted a hard-line stance toward the forces he himself had unleashed. In the autumn of 1990 he ousted all his liberal advisers and appointed the party "concrete" in their stead. Thus, Alexander Yakovlev, Roy Medvedev, and other leading figures of perestroika left the government to make room for Boris Pugo, Genady Yanayev, and such. The "crawling coup" was denounced by Eduard Shevardnadze, the last reformer still left in the Gorbachev government, before he quit the Foreign Ministry in December 1990. Rumors of the forthcoming coup intensified, with the assault on the Baltics in January 1991 closely following the 1981 scenario of martial law in Poland.

It soon became clear, however, that Gorbachev was incapable of delivering a forceful solution. This was true for many reasons, including changes in society that already had taken place during the glasnost years. Yet at that stage the Communist Party of the Soviet Union, its sorry state notwithstanding, was not beyond rescue. The loss of membership did not have to be damaging. The Leninist party is elitist by nature and at its best when in a state of siege; a hostile environment enhances its internal discipline and helps to differentiate real Bolsheviks from impostors. And many "real Bolsheviks" were left in the Soviet republics, though they were more likely to be in their sixties than in their thirties. The CPSU might yet have relived its days of glory, chasing revisionists from its ranks and claiming the superiority of the Soviet system over all other forms of government, had it not been for the failure to gain the army's support.

When the rehearsal of the martial law scenario in the Baltics began in January 1991, with local "salvation fronts" being activated and troops being dispatched to capture strategic sites in the cities, Gorbachev appeared to lack cannons. The Soviet army, after being persecuted, sneered at, and spat on during the five years of Gorbachev's perestroika, showed unwillingness, inability, or both, to continue fighting on his orders. Several analysts already had pointed to a problem in Gorbachev's tactics of undermining the army at the time of ethnic unrest. To understand this failing, another conflict underpinning the logistics of perestroika, the KGB-military contest, needs to be considered.

Chapter 3

Vertical Disintegration:
The KGB-Military Contest

We had won and no one—not even the KGB officer—seemed (to be) afraid any more.—Oleg Kalugin, former general of the KGB commenting on the failure of the August 1991 coup

The debate on the nature of power relations within the ruling Soviet troika, party-KGB-army, has been inconclusive. Roughly, two general assumptions can be distinguished. The first, which came from the totalitarian model, conceived of the Soviet center as relatively homogeneous and consolidated by a common interest in maintaining the power base at home and expansion abroad. Such an approach was best represented by Mikhail Voslensky's concept of nomenklatura. He showed how the procedures and practices of promotion within the apparatus of power created the self-perpetuating Soviet elite. In Voslensky's view, this elite was essentially coherent, and such institutions as the army and the KGB were effectively harnessed in the service of the party.

The second model was initiated by Roman Kolkowicz's analyses of Soviet civil-military relations.[1] It stressed the latent conflict between party and army, which culminated from time to time in violent clashes, such as Stalin's bloody purges of the officer corps or Khrushchev's rough treatment of his defense minister, Georgy Zhukov. Having received decisive help from the military twice in his career, against Lavrenty Beria in 1953 and then against the "antiparty group"[2] in 1962, Khrushchev made it clear that the army's role as kingmaker was to end. In fact, it did not. The part taken by the military in the removal of Khrushchev is still disputed.[3] In the mid-sixties, however, the support of the defense

minister, Marshal Andrei Grechko, became a decisive factor behind Brezhnev's victory over his opponents in the Politburo.[4]
Considering their mutual enmity, Kolkowicz wrote, the "relationship between the Communist Party and the Soviet military
is essentially conflict-prone and thus presents a perennial threat
to the political stability of the Soviet state."[5] Nevertheless, under
Brezhnev's leadership smooth cooperation between the army and
the party continued well into the seventies, which gave rise to
some revisions in the "conflict model."

Kolkowicz's analysis was criticized by William Odom, who
pointed to certain features of the Soviet army that made its political role markedly different from that of the military under other
dictatorships. First and foremost, the Soviet military could not
dispense with communist ideology, which made its relations with
the party symbiotic rather than conflictual, occasional differences
of opinion between them notwithstanding.[6] According to Odom,
the party and the army had more common interests than opposing ones, which made the Soviet regime more stable than the
conflict model would suggest.

One insider view of the Soviet army reconciles both models,
one stressing conflict, the other based on consensus.[7] According
to Viktor Suvorov, a former officer in Soviet military counterintelligence (GRU), the stability of the post-Stalinist regime depended
on a three-corner game within the ruling troika: the party, the
army, and the KGB. Since none of the actors was powerful enough
to win over the combined powers of the other two, the balance of
powers depended on shifting alliances within the triangle. Whenever one player was in danger of becoming too strong, the other
two colluded to bring him down. After Stalin's death, when the
KGB threatened both the party and the army, it was crushed by
the alliance made by Khrushchev and Zhukov. When, in turn, the
military was growing too powerful, Khrushchev revitalized the
weakened KGB to curb Marshal Zhukov's Napoleonic ambitions.
Suvorov's "tripoid" model allows for both conflict and consensus
in party-military relations, depending on the current configuration within the triangle.

Other interpretations were based on direct parallels with civil-military relations in the Western countries. According to Samuel P. Huntington, the development of modern warfare altogether changed the mode of civilian control over the military.[8] The traditional or "subjective" mode of control that relies on direct civilian interference inside the army has become counterproductive in maintaining the efficiency of a modern defense system. The modern pattern of civilian control has become less intrusive. Thus, the new, "objective" mode of civilian-military relations in the developed countries was established, based on a civilian government's recognition of the military's professional autonomy, on the one hand, and on compliance by the military with the civilian primacy in politics, on the other.

Some specialists perceived a similar pattern developing in the Soviet bloc.[9] Such an approach was well attuned to a larger framework of "corporatist" and "interest groups" explanations of the Brezhnev regime, under which the Soviet military, very much like other organized interest groups, was allowed some autonomy within its professional sphere and was able to defend its "corporate" interests.[10] It seems doubtful, though, whether a concept of "civilian control" culled from the West could have been applied directly to Soviet civil-military relations.

True, the military's position under the Soviet regime was less dominant than in other dictatorships, but the party alone (being the Soviet counterpart of a "civilian" government) had never been able to control the army sufficiently, not even by elaborate methods of indoctrination and internal screening. The only effective control of the Soviet military had been exercised by the political police, that is, the KGB and its predecessors. Indeed, for the greatest part of its existence, the Soviet Union was a police state, and that was why a military takeover was highly unlikely. This fact, however, is not sufficient to make Huntington's model of objective civilian control relevant to the Soviet regime.

First, the Soviet military always resented KGB intrusions into its affairs, and it tried to challenge them whenever it was in a position to do so. Thus, a mutual recognition of the spheres of influence in civil-military relations, typical of the objective mode of control, was far from being stable. Second, KGB control over the army could be called "civilian" in a sense, provided the party was fully in control of the KGB. The main thesis to be substantiated in this chapter is that the party was not in full control.

The Question of an Alternative Elite

As often happens, developments in the Soviet Union went well beyond all the concepts presented above. Toward the mid-1970s the military's strength was increasing to an extent that suggested its future predominance in the Soviet power structure. In 1976 Michel Tatu, an analyst of Soviet affairs, concluded that the supreme Soviet leader was "no longer in a position to take any important decision that runs counter to the opinion of the military."[11] Zbigniew Brzezinski went even further, predicting that, as things looked at that time, the scenario of a Soviet marshal one day mounting the podium as the party's new secretary general could not be excluded. He credited this possibility to the fact that "no other elite group in the Soviet Union [was] capable either of supporting the Party in the event of a major crisis, or of replacing the Party in the event the crisis should get out of hand."[12]

Brzezinski's prognosis actually materialized in Poland, when General Wojciech Jaruzelski became first secretary as a result of the Solidarity crisis. It did not, however, take hold in the Soviet Union. On the contrary, the army's role in the last and lethal Soviet crisis was passive. To understand this development, a third actor that had not been given an independent role and agenda in the Western debate on Soviet civil-military relations, that is, the KGB, should be included in the analysis. For the KGB also had aspired to become an "alternative elite," and, up to a point, it was more successful than the military in fulfilling this ambition. It was a KGB general, and not an army general, who mounted the podium as general secretary in December 1982 in the person of Yuri Andropov. The decade and a half preceding this event had been marked by an increasing emancipation from party control of both the KGB and the military.

The turning point for the Soviet military came in the spring of 1967 with the death of the defense minister, Marshal Rodion Malinowsky. A new appointment was delayed for twelve days, during which time the decision had to be taken whether his successor should be a civilian or a military professional. The stalemate was resolved in favor of the officer corps. The appointment of Marshal Grechko opened the golden age of the Soviet military. Grechko's strong personality supplied the army with decisive leadership that had been lacking since Zhukov's demotion. The power of the military was rapidly increasing by the end of the sixties and it continued to grow in the seventies.

There were two manifestations of this military dominance. First of all, the army had gradually taken control of a substantial and most valuable part of the Soviet economy. In 1968 the military-industrial complex acquired uniform structures throughout the Soviet bloc in the form of defense councils, created in all satellite states. For a long time analysts have recognized that the Soviet economy was primarily directed toward military needs. Nevertheless, the size of the military-industrial complex came to be known only recently; it has been assessed as more than 70 percent of the Soviet Union's productive forces. Today it is deemed the main obstacle to market reforms in Russia. Second, the general staff concentrated under its command all paramilitary forces such as the border troops and the MVD (ordinary police) formations. Further, the army took over from the KGB the custody of nuclear charges as well as the responsibility for transporting them.[13] In a symbolic gesture KGB forces had become subject to conscription as part of the biannual call-up by the Ministry of Defense.

Crucial for party control over both forces was the Central Committee Administrative Department, where all appointments and promotions to both military and KGB ranks were made. Thus, successive appointments of heads of this department were subject to fierce competition and reflected the shifts of power relations within the ruling troika. A few days after Khrushchev's down-

fall, his man in charge of the Administrative Department, Nikolai Mironov, was killed in a plane crash during a trip to Yugoslavia. His position was taken over by Vladimir Semishchastny,
the former KGB chairman, who kept it until he was demoted in
1967. "The delicate nature of the position is shown by the difficulty the collective leadership that took over from Khrushchev
had in agreeing on a successor [to head the Administrative De-
partment]."[14] The appointment of Nikolai Savinkin, a man with
a military-political background, was a sign that the army of Marshal Grechko was taking a substantial degree of control over military appointments and promotions. Thus, the devices that enabled the party to exercise internal control over the military had
become the responsibility of the military itself.

A similar pattern of appropriating an agency that was supposed
to secure party control over the military could be observed in the
case of the Main Political Administration (MPA). The MPA had
its political directorates attached to all military commands in the
person of a political commissar as a deputy commander. The way
in which this powerful instrument of political control, devised by
Trotsky, was falling increasingly into military hands has been described by Timothy Colton.[15]

Stalin drew from the pool of political commissars when he had
to compensate for the losses in the officer corps that resulted from
his purges of 1938.[16] The ranks of political officers, in turn, were
filled with civilian party workers. After 1958 a distinct reversal
of this policy occurred. The political officers tended to be drawn
from a pool of the professional military. This meant increasing
militarization of the MPA. Shortly before this practice was officially forbidden in the early 1960s, almost half of all political
officers were former commanders. Regardless of the change in
official policy, however, the jobs of political officers gradually had
switched from external surveillance of the officer corps to military administration, helping professional officers to raise combat
readiness and reinforce discipline. The political officers came to
be considered professional soldiers with specialized training and
lifetime commitment to the service.[17]

In other words, the MPA came under military sway. A favorite preoccupation of analysts of the Soviet press became detecting the recurrent disagreements revealed between the lines of *Pravda* editorials representing the current party line and those of the MPA daily, *Krasnaya Zvezda,* that clearly represented the military standpoint. Several attempts were made to bring the MPA under more effective party supervision, but they failed.[18] In the end, the usual "subjective" methods of party control over the military had become more theoretical than real.

Police control was the only effective method that the party was able to exercise over the army. The KGB provided the ultimate defense against subversion in the military through its Third Chief Directorate of so-called Special Departments, which were responsible for military counterintelligence. Special Departments had a tradition, reaching back to the 1937–38 purges, of exercising punitive powers in the army. Thus, the crucial question is: how effective was KGB control over the army? And no less important: how effective was the party's control of the KGB? Generally, KGB control over the army was increasing while party control over the KGB was weakening.

Again, personalities proved decisive. After the humiliation suffered under Khrushchev, the KGB wasted a first chance of improving its position following his ousting in 1964. The then KGB chair, Semishchastny, did not have much political experience, having been promoted to the post directly from Komsomol leadership. This appointment was just another symptom of the KGB's bad political standing at the time. Only in 1967 with the appointment of Yuri Andropov, who at the time made an unimposing figure as head of the CC department for contacts with communist parties, did the military find a real competitor.

Andropov was a bright man, a relative rarity among the nomenklatura after the brain drain it suffered in the Great Purge when Lenin's "professional revolutionaries" were replaced by Stalin's "country bumpkins." "In a way, I always thought Andropov was the most dangerous of all of them, simply because he was smarter than the rest," said an experienced apparatchik from Leonid Brezhnev's nomenklatura and subsequently one of Gorbachev's advisers.[19] Andropov had yet another personal advantage over his fellow apparatchiks—a talent for public relations. Under his leadership the public image of the KGB steadily improved after the damage done to it by Khrushchev's speech to the Twentieth Party Congress in 1956. Writers were hired by the dozen, and a flood of literature glorifying Chekist heroes appeared. The cult of Felix Dzerzhinsky was resumed. Although Andropov himself rescinded an open terror that was typical of his hero, he understood the significance of the founding father for maintaining the KGB's internal morale and external stature.

It was not until 1978 that the KGB's formal status rose from that of a modest committee attached to the Council of Ministers to become a state committee of the USSR, that is, a full ministry. More important than formal status, though, was the quality of the institution. In the opinion of former CIA director Stansfield Turner, Andropov's KGB became "a very well run and excellently managed agency."[20] That was more than could be said of many other Soviet institutions, and it provided Andropov with an additional edge in the ensuing contest for the top leadership.

From Balance to Contest

Brezhnev achieved a remarkable stability of the regime by bringing the KGB-military contest to a draw. Both Grechko and Andropov became full members of the Politburo in 1973. But for at least two reasons the regime's stability was only temporary. First, army and KGB leaders both strove not for balance but for domination over one another. Second, maintaining a balance of power between the KGB and the army depended on the party's proper management of their rivalry. To perform the role of a superarbiter, however, the party itself had to be consolidated. As the party apparatus fragmented over time (see chapter 2), some of its sections became involved in the internecine struggle between the very forces that the party was supposed to control.

Particular factions within the party apparatus allied themselves with either the military or the KGB. As a rule, the regional leaders had been "drafted" onto the military side, whereas the central departments came under the sway of the KGB (with the exception of the military-industrial sector). The Ministry of Foreign Affairs under Andrei Gromyko had closely cooperated with the KGB. Foreign policy became the stage of KGB-military confrontations in the mid-seventies. Andropov built up a remarkable foreign department, where sophisticated new methods of espionage were developed. As a result, the KGB came to possess a large information base abroad. Andropov also bolstered the position of civilian experts in matters of defense. His patronage of the Institute of the USA and Canada, chaired by Georgy Arbatov, and the Institute of World Economy and International Relations, directed by Inozemtsov, was well known, both men having been former Andropov employees in his Central Committee department. In the mid-1970s civilian experts from those institutions began to play an increasing role in the deliberations over military choices.

Tension always had existed between the two tracks of Soviet foreign policy. Historically, the first track was ideological and had a messianic objective, which coincided with the imperial reflex toward territorial expansion in various guises. The second track was pragmatic, based on the doctrine of peaceful coexistence, which supported ongoing Soviet negotiations with the West. The benefit of negotiations with the capitalists was recurrently questioned by the military, which considered such talks too demanding in terms of the concessions required and ultimately ineffective. The military position was simple: instead of searching for détente, the Soviet Union should do its best to keep up with the U.S. military buildup at whatever cost. When faced with imminent defeat in the technological race precipitated by U.S. President Ronald Reagan's Star Wars, the most active sections of the Soviet military seemed to be in favor of immediate confrontation rather than any change in security strategy or doctrine. For example, Chief of General Staff N. V. Ogarkov in a series of pamphlets and articles advanced an aggressive position toward the American challenge in the arms race.[21]

Diplomatic means were defended by Gromyko, whose experience in negotiating with the West was enormous. His was a tenacious diplomacy, most often passive and negative, of the wait-and-see type. Gromyko's memoirs reveal a colorless functionary with a sober judgment, derived from the Leninist calculation of the correlation of forces, complete with the orthodoxy of class struggle, which justified a nihilistic approach in relations with the capitalist world.[22] Gromyko made his ministry a formidable institution. His assets were longevity in the service and the expertise necessary to negotiations. He focused his policy on the United States, and his aim was détente. Andropov's civilian experts supported Gromyko in defending the SALT I Treaty, which the army staunchly opposed.

A more sophisticated version of peaceful coexistence was developed by Andropov when, as chair of the KGB, he elaborated an array of active measures abroad. He was in favor of a more flexible diplomacy, open to "reasonable compromises," especially on the issue of human rights. Andropov also supported broader contacts with people and organizations in the West, sometimes handled directly and sometimes indirectly by his institution. Apart from the traditional support for the Western antiwar movements, other concerns of postindustrial societies, such as the problems of environmental pollution, regional conflicts, poverty, and development, were also addressed by the KGB's head as useful in Soviet foreign policy. All of these themes were to be found later on Gorbachev's agenda.

The military received support from the hard core of the regional party apparatus: the first secretaries of Moscow (Viktor Grishin) and Leningrad (Grigory Romanov) and the Ukrainian party leader, Vladimir Shcherbitsky, all had seats in the Politburo and supported the tough foreign policy options.[23] In return, the military hard-liners were forthcoming in regard to local cooperation between the military district commanders and the republican and regional party committees, which was a sensitive issue and the subject of a long-standing controversy. Stalin took unusual precautions to see that the military and party hierarchies did not mingle, but from the mid-sixties several republican committees included local military representatives. By the mid-eighties, however, KGB representation in the regional party committees was double the representation from the army.[24]

Negotiations for the SALT I Treaty gathered speed only after the unexpected death of Grechko in 1976 and the removal of the chief of general staff, Marshal Victor Kuligov, a few months later. The new minister of defense, Konstantin Ustinov, was a civilian who showed a much more open attitude toward arms control than his predecessor. A popular opinion was that Ustinov represented party interests in the army rather than the other way round. Nevertheless, at that stage the army still constituted a considerable political force, as seen in the invasion of Afghanistan that put a stop to the SALT II negotiations in 1978.[25] In retrospect, however, this invasion seems to have been the swan song of the Soviet military in its quest for political expansion.

The Turning Point: What to Do About Poland?

The decisive moment in the KGB-military contest came in the autumn of 1980. At that time, developments in Poland made a real difference to power relations in the Kremlin. The post of the general secretary of the CPSU was at stake. Brezhnev was already terminally ill, and the decision on what to do about Poland would determine his successor.

The military solution, had it been adopted, would have strengthened the hands of the army generals and that section of the party apparatus associated with them. Invasions usually had boosted the military's political status. After the Hungarian invasion the Soviet generals recovered from the "Stalinist complex," and General Georgy Zhukov became increasingly assertive. The invasion of Czechoslovakia in 1968 initiated the golden age of the Soviet military under the leadership of General Grechko.

The invasion of Afghanistan in 1979 had a lesser impact because of the problems it brought: the military had managed to stop the SALT II negotiations, but a prolonged war with few prospects for a quick victory made the army politically vulnerable. The invasion of Poland, had it been undertaken, would have moved the military back to the center of the Soviet political stage. For the same reason it would have been a major setback for the KGB and Andropov's plans for the succession.

In retrospect, it can be said that had the Soviet military succeeded in swaying the Politburo toward the invasion of Poland in 1980–81, Andropov would have had little chance of becoming general secretary, and, instead of Gorbachev's perestroika, the Soviet Union would have received a military dictatorship. This possibility is why the developments of that period deserve the utmost attention.

Martial law, imposed on Poland by General Wojciech Jaruzelski on 13 December 1981, has been the subject of a lengthy controversy. The general and his comrades from the Military Council for National Salvation always have presented their case as the lesser of two evils; had they not introduced the state of war (so-called according to the Polish constitution of that time), a Soviet invasion would have been unavoidable. Traditionally, Poles have been extremely sensitive to arguments of raison d'état. If Jaruzelski's claim to be acting in Poland's best interests had been credible, he would have received massive support. This had happened twenty-five years earlier when Władysław Gomułka convinced Khrushchev that Polish communists could manage without "fraternal" help, thereby delivering Poland from the threat of Soviet invasion, which won Gomułka the blessing of the Polish Catholic bishops. Jaruzelski, however, was not very convincing in his role as savior; it was commonly felt that he represented the best interest of the Soviet Union in Poland rather than the other way round. These feelings received some confirmation when the Soviet archives were opened.

While a post-1989 special parliamentary commission was deliberating in Poland on the rights and wrongs of Jaruzelski and his generals, documents arriving from the former Soviet archives threw more light on the matter. The most important were transcripts of CPSU Politburo meetings, top-secret communications between Brezhnev and Jaruzelski, and internal documents of the

CPSU Central Committee, all of which have appeared in various publications.[26] These documents indicated that at the critical time when martial law was about to be introduced, the firm resolve of the Brezhnev Politburo was *not to send troops to Poland.* What is more, from deliberations at the Soviet Politburo held on 10 December 1981, two days before the critical date, one may conclude that Jaruzelski actively sought an assurance from the Soviet leadership that, should the Polish army fail to do the job, "fraternal" help would arrive from the Soviet Union:

Rusakov: [Jaruzelski] says that if the Polish forces are unable to cope with the resistance put up by "Solidarity," the Polish comrades hope to receive assistance from other countries, up to and including the introduction of armed forces on the territory of Poland. Jaruzelski is basing this hope on the speech by Comrade Kulikov [chief commander of the Warsaw Pact], who reportedly said that the USSR and other socialist countries would indeed give assistance to Poland with their armed forces.[27]

Thus, Jaruzelski was less anxious to avoid the Soviet invasion than he was afraid that no invasion would take place, and, should anything go wrong, he and his comrades would find themselves in a difficult position.

At the beginning of the crisis, Jaruzelski's preferences were for the joint forces of the Warsaw Pact to solve the problem, with the exclusion of German troops (for historical reasons), but with Polish troops included.[28] The Soviet scenario for invasion was different, however. The Soviet side had no qualms about including the Germans—and Erich Honecker was more than eager to oblige[29]—but the Polish army was considered unpredictable and therefore the prime target of, rather than a participant in, military operations.[30] Nevertheless, the preference for an "internal solution" of the Polish problem clearly had prevailed among the Soviet leadership, so much so that Jaruzelski was firmly rebuffed when he hinted that Soviet troops might be useful after all.

Andropov: [Jaruzelski] is raising the question, albeit indirectly, of receiving military assistance as well [on top of economic assistance]. . . .

If comrade Kulikov actually did speak about the introduction of troops, then I believe he did this incorrectly. We can't risk such a step. We don't intend to introduce troops into Poland. That is the proper position, and we must adhere to it until the end. I don't know how things will turn out in Poland, but even if Poland falls under the control of "Solidarity," that's the way it will be.[31]

This was the most radical position taken at the meeting against invasion. Although all participants expressed the same opinion in the matter (referring to the previous decision made by Brezhnev), none of them went so far as to say that, no matter what happened in Poland—even if Solidarity won the forthcoming confrontation—there would be no Soviet military intervention.

Mark Kramer has analyzed this unusual Soviet policy toward one of the most important satellites and makes four major points. First, the Soviet leadership had always viewed military action as a last-ditch option, to be used only after all other measures failed. Second, all other invasions were aimed against wayward Communist Party leaders, whereas the top levels of the Polish communist hierarchy and the military leadership remained loyal to Moscow throughout the eighteen-month crisis, so that an invasion would have had to be directed against the entire Polish population rather than against a well-defined target at the top. Third, the risks involved in invading Poland, with its population of nearly 40 million and a record of putting up a good fight before surrendering, were much greater than they had been with much smaller Hungary or Czechoslovakia, not to mention problems posed by subsequent "normalization." Finally, the Soviet leadership would have intervened no matter what if the situation in Poland had spun out of hand, and Andropov's statement about not sending troops, even if Poland fell under the control of Solidarity, was clearly an anomaly.

Having considered all these elements, Kramer concluded that the "Soviet leadership's pursuit of an 'internal solution' to the Polish crisis was by no means a departure from its responses to previous crises in Eastern Europe"; anyway, no proof exists that the Soviets would have given up Poland for good.[32] One may agree with this last of Kramer's opinions. It seems doubtful that the Soviet decision not to invade was tantamount to giving up Poland altogether. Yet it is more difficult to accept his argument to the effect that the decision of the Soviet Politburo, as documented in the materials presented in his article, was not unusual. This decision was a clear deviation from previous Soviet policy toward the satellites, especially a country as strategically placed as Poland.

First, no evidence indicates that all previous Soviet decisions to invade were taken as "last-ditch measures." Had the Czechs and Slovaks been given as much warning about what was going to happen to them in August 1968 as the Poles were given during eighteen months of their Solidarity freedom festival, the need to invade Czechoslovakia would not have arisen. The invasion of Czechoslovakia was by no means a "last-ditch measure"; on the contrary, it caught both the Czech party leadership and the Czech people by surprise. The Soviet decision to invade in 1968 was taken because the Soviet military was strong enough to make it happen and not because all other measures had been exhausted.[33] The invasion of Hungary, on the other hand, was a case of a last-ditch measure, because the country would have been lost to the Soviet bloc had it not been invaded. But the Hungarian problem was not so much a question of dissenting leadership—Imre Nagy was amply prepared to compromise—as a popular revolution, differing from Poland in 1980 only in that the Hungarians were armed. This difference, however, was hardly to Poland's advantage.

True, the problems posed by a Polish invasion would have been greater than they had been in Hungary or Czechoslovakia and there is no doubt that the "normalization" process also would have been more difficult. But the problem was not one of skirmishes between two neighboring countries; it was about a superpower and its wayward satellite. The Soviet Union was certain of winning a war with Poland, should one occur, and the stakes were such that the other problems quoted by Kramer would have had to come second. The Soviet leadership had not spent decades building up its offensive capacity to match that of NATO, only to give up its most important strategic position on the Western front while the cold war was still on. In other words, the Soviet leadership would have much preferred keeping Poland by peaceful means rather than by waging war. But where Soviet interests were concerned, invasion would have seemed a "lesser evil."

But who was to define Soviet interests at that time? The party, headed by the ailing Brezhnev, already was torn by succession struggles. The military and the KGB were the main contenders. Trying to make sense of the Soviet leadership's decisions without regard to the succession contest already under way is like trying to understand a soccer match while ignoring the position of the ball.

Furthermore, taking into consideration the conflicting interests of factions involved in the Soviet succession struggle, it is easier to understand why Andropov's determination not to invade was greater than that of others attending the Politburo meeting; the decision to invade would have put the trump cards in the hands of his military rivals and robbed Andropov of the objective toward which he had been striving for nearly a decade—the position of general secretary of the CPSU.

How Andropov Saved Poland

The unsolved riddle is: how did he do it? How did Andropov manage to avoid an obvious decision of the Soviet leadership to invade Poland when communism was collapsing in that country? How did he stop the Soviet generals from doing what they felt was the only thing to do? The following attempt to shed light on this puzzle is based largely on analyses of unusual personnel changes in the Soviet ground forces during the critical period of December 1980–March 1981.[34]

Shortly after Solidarity's official registration on 16 November 1980, *Krasnaya Zvezda* (the Soviet military paper) was in high spirits, running an article on the Polish-Soviet war of 1920. It concluded with Lenin's words: "The war with Poland is forced upon us."[35] The Warsaw Pact countries were at the height of readiness to invade at least twice: in December 1980 and in March 1981.[36] Each time the operation was called off. Some circumstances of those reversals were described by the then Polish first secretary, Stanislaw Kania, in his memoirs. On 5 December 1980, after long discussions held in Moscow, Brezhnev told Kania, "We are not coming."[37] In March 1981, in the tense situation with the forthcoming general strike in Poland, Kania received a similar pledge at a secret meeting with Andropov. By that time Andropov was well able to give such an assurance. Between December 1980 and March 1981 the military faction driving toward the invasion of Poland had been neutralized by a series of reassignments in the top positions of the ground forces.

The ground forces were subordinated to twenty territorial commands inside the USSR and the groups of forces situated in East Germany, Poland, Czechoslovakia, and Hungary. The series of reassignments started at the beginning of December 1980 with the removal of the commander-in-chief, General Pavlovsky and his political deputy, General Vasyagin. By mid-January 1981 all the military districts bordering on Poland, except one, had changed either their commanders or their political deputies, or both. These were the most senior posts in the military establishment below the general staff level, and they were filled with obscure generals brought most often from remote Far Eastern military districts. Later on, such replacements became a favorite Gorbachev maneuver.

If Soviet ground forces were ordered to be ready to move to Poland by 15 December as U.S. intelligence indicated, it was a peculiar time for the induction of commanders lacking experience in the area to the army's most operational posts. The official rationale for the shake-up came in 1981.[38] Apparently serious problems were involved with the mobilization of forces. In particular, reservists called up for the emergency to their divisions in the Carpathian Military District were deserting in such numbers that it was impossible to punish them. The Carpathian district covered the western Ukraine adjoining the Polish border. However, this military district was the only one located along the Polish border where the command had been left intact during the recent series of reassignments.[39] It would seem extraordinary that disturbances in the Carpathian district should prompt a shake-up throughout the entire ground forces, while the command of this district remained the only one left unaffected. Yet that is what happened.

The situation becomes clearer on examining the changes that took place in the Carpathian district a few months earlier. A new chief of the district's political directorate was appointed in August 1980 at the time when the Polish crisis began.[40] In light of further developments one might conjecture that the reports of "mass desertion of recruits" in this district, a highly unlikely phenomenon in the Soviet army, were probably fabricated as an excuse for the turmoil in the ground forces, and it is possible that these personnel changes prevented the invasion of Poland.

The Export of Cadres

Andropov's major advantage over his military opponents was that the KGB had the capacity, indeed a long-standing tradition, of placing its own people in sensitive posts in other institutions.[41] The export of cadres was Andropov's most effective method of taking control of crucial developments. At first, the main targets were the territorial party apparatus and the MVD (the ordinary and criminal police). With the MVD's help, Andropov was able to compromise and then prosecute corrupt republican leaders.[42] In the late 1970s some MVD and KGB republican chairmen became first secretaries—for example, Geidar Aliyev in Azerbaijan and Eduard Shevardnadze in Georgia. Voslensky has suggested that these republican takeovers, preceded by local anticorruption campaigns, were rehearsals for the scenario that was eventually applied in the center. When the moment came, Andropov did not hesitate to threaten even the Brezhnev family in order to intimidate the entire party leadership into supporting his candidacy for general secretary.[43]

A vital position in controlling the succession struggle was that of the Kremlin's chief physician, Yevgeny Chazov, who held that position in the critical years of Brezhnev's deteriorating health. In his memoirs Chazov makes no secret of his allegiance to Andropov.[44] When it became clear to Chazov in the mid-seventies that Brezhnev was terminally ill and his condition rapidly deteriorating, Andropov was the first to receive this vital information. Chazov, while keeping the secret from his rivals for some time, also made sure that Andropov was the first to learn about Brezhnev's death.

A gradual takeover by Andropov of the most precious instrument of party rule, the right of appointment to political administrative posts, made the KGB and the party almost two branches of the same organization, with the KGB branch becoming increasingly influential. The fact that the KGB was able to control vital party operations was another symptom of the predicament of the party apparatus and the prime cause of its losing the struggle for succession after Brezhnev.

As the control of political appointments was being gradually diverted from the party to the KGB Andropov was able to support the careers of the ablest regional secretaries in the central party apparatus. It was, in fact, the only patronage network for ambitious younger cadres (Gorbachev being one of them) who were kept in the cold by the Brezhnev gerontocracy. Thus, Andropov took advantage of Brezhnev's golden rule of the stability of cadres in building up his following in the party apparatus.

How Andropov's patronage network operated can be seen in the promotion of Gorbachev from the Stavropol province to the Central Committee Secretariat in 1978. After the death of the CC secretary for agriculture, Fyodor Kulakov, the competing candidates for the post were Medunov from the Krasnodar region and Mikhail Gorbachev from Stavropol. Since, as a rule, subsequent promotions to the Central Committee were made from other than neighboring provinces, the loser in this competition would have no other opportunity for advancement for a long time. The position of secretary for agriculture was vacant for more than three months, and the important part in the decision-making process was played by Andropov.

A significant factor in his strategy was where Brezhnev spent his holidays. At first, he went to Sochi, which was in Medunov's territory. But in the decisive period for the appointment in question, Brezhnev's physician recommended the northern Caucasus spas, which were in Gorbachev's oblast. Andropov arranged Brezhnev's visit to Kislovodzk. At a small railway station, Mineralne Vody, the famous meeting took place between the four men who soon would succeed each other as party leaders: Brezhnev, Andropov, Chernenko, and Gorbachev.[45] Andropov also mobilized the help of Mikhail Suslov, who himself had been promoted from the Stavropol party committee and personally disliked Medunov and his mafia.[46]

When the time of succession came, Andropov had a network of his own men in the provincial committees who saw in him the promise of further promotion. Unlike other leaders, he needed little time to consolidate his powers. The first statement of policy under the Andropov leadership was signed with his name instead of being the usual collective statement of the CC and the Politburo: "It was an authoritative statement by a man who felt free to speak as the leader."[47] Jerry Hough explained the speed with which Andropov solidified his position as resulting from the "institutionalization of the post of General Secretary." The very fact, however, that the struggle for succession was lost to the KGB was a sign of the decline and degeneration of the party apparatus rather than its growing strength, let alone its "institutionalization." A more obvious explanation of the firmness with which Andropov took over leadership is that he built up his following during his time as KGB chair.

The death of Andropov and the election of Chernenko was not a setback for the KGB. In that period the important question of succession in the Defense Ministry was decided. Dmitri Ustinov was seriously ill, and the successor most preferred by the military was the chief of general staff, General Nikolai Ogarkov. Ogarkov was the most outspoken defender of the military's interests and one of its ablest professionals. He had just expressed his apprehension in the military press about the state of readiness of the Soviet army, comparing it with the situation on the eve of

World War II.[48] The best proof that Andropov, despite the brief period of his rule, had actually managed to undercut the political influence of the Soviet military for good was that Chernenko removed Ogarkov from the general staff before the authoritative general could have a say in choosing the new defense minister. Ustinov's successor was Marshal Sokolov, who never received full Politburo membership.

When Chernenko died in 1985, "the Military, lacking either a civilian or professional military representative in the Politburo, was ill-equipped to exert a significant influence over the Party's choice" of the next leader.[49] That the KGB was on the winning side with the accession of Gorbachev was clear from the program adopted by the Twenty-Seventh Party Congress in 1986. In this program, political security was ranked as equally important to military might, something that had not happened before in the post-Stalinist period.

From such an enhanced position the All-Union KGB was able to confront some of its republican headquarters that had gone "native." This was especially the case with the Ukrainian KGB, firmly under the control of the long-standing republican party leader, Vladimir Shcherbitsky, who had managed to survive Gorbachev's purges and keep his membership of the Politburo until 1989, his open hostility toward perestroika notwithstanding. He was removed only after the Ukrainian KGB was compromised by a series of affairs investigated from Moscow. In 1987 the "Berkhin affair" broke.[50] It was the case of a journalist persecuted for his investigation of a high-level corruption case in the Ukraine. It gave the then KGB chairman, Viktor Chebrikov, an opportunity to condemn the illegal methods of the Ukrainian KGB. Next was the "Odessa affair," where local KGB investigators were accused of fabricating bribery charges against an innocent MVD officer. The American scholar Amy Knight described these developments as "a heavy blow to KGB authority." But the blow was much more damaging to Shcherbitsky's authority in the Ukraine than to KGB headquarters in Moscow.

Gorbachev and the KGB

Conspicuous KGB support for Gorbachev made some commentators look for a conspiracy behind perestroika. For example, Victor Yasman of Radio Liberty pointed out that "the KGB is the only institution with any experience of working in anything resembling conditions of glasnost," owing to its experience in espionage in liberal democratic countries.[51] Other researchers were surprised "to find the secret police intimately involved in the origins of perestroika."[52]

A theory of the KGB conspiring with Gorbachev to free the Soviet people from the evil of Stalinism is, of course, too far-reaching. On the other hand, the image of Gorbachev struggling single-handedly with the entire Soviet establishment seems just as naive. He certainly needed the support of some significant forces within the regime, and the fact that he received that support from the KGB can hardly be disputed. In the opinion of the last KGB chair, Vadim Bakatin, "Gorbachev . . . saw in the KGB not so much a danger to his reforms as a support for them."[53]

To put things in proper perspective, it first should be noted that Gorbachev operated within the personnel network bestowed on him by his late patron, Yuri Andropov. This provided the newly appointed general secretary with a great deal of his initial strength but also imposed certain limitations on his actions later on. Andropov's network, inherited by Gorbachev, consisted of at least two different groups. The first one came from the party apparatus and the KGB/MVD ranks, with men such as Vladimir Kruchkov, Yegor Ligachev, Eduard Shevardnadze, Nikolai Ryzhkov, Geidar Aliyev, etc. These officials were all experienced operators of the Brezhnev machinery of power for whom perestroika meant their turn at the wheel. The second group consisted of the party intellectuals, such as Alexander Yakovlev, Yuri Afanasyev, Georgy Shakhnazarov, Georgy Arbatov, Fedor Burlatsky, Bovin, Gerasimov, and others, whose task it was to provide the ideological framework for perestroika.

Predictably enough, the two groups soon parted company, the intellectuals becoming increasingly radical and the apparatus more conservative. Gorbachev followed his radical advisers, while skillfully protecting his rear among the more conservative apparatchiks. But the balance was difficult to maintain. Since the radicals apparently had more to offer in terms of mobilizing popular support for perestroika at home and wide applause abroad, Gorbachev gave them the upper hand; at the nineteenth party conference in the summer of 1988, the breakneck program of democratization at home and New Thinking abroad was adopted. Before this happened, however, Gorbachev had to overcome the vestiges of resistance left in the military establishment.

Gorbachev Finishes Off the Soviet Military

If Andropov's strategy was to curb the military's political ambitions, Gorbachev's agenda was far more radical. Whatever his intentions, Gorbachev certainly helped make the world a safer place by undermining its greatest menace—the Soviet army. Gorbachev's motives behind this extraordinary undertaking have been explained by his New Thinking and by domestic—mainly economic—concerns. Those concerns were real enough, but, as has been argued at length in chapter 2, they were not sufficient to explain either perestroika or the New Thinking. New Thinking theory by itself is a tautology, since such a sea change in the Soviet perception of the outside world needs to be separately explained. Part of this explanation has been suggested in chapter 1 in the wider context of a generational change among the Soviet political elite. The consequences of that shift in Soviet foreign policy will be discussed in more detail in chapter 4. Here, only two of the possible reasons for Gorbachev's policy toward the military will be outlined.

First, Gorbachev's stance on the military was to some extent determined by the very logic of his factional struggle; the military was connected to the section of the apparatus that he was fighting

—the party bosses of the largest republics (Vladimir Shcherbitsky from the Ukraine and Dinmuhammed Kunayev from Kazakhstan) and the cities (Georgy Romanov of Leningrad and Viktor Grishin of Moscow), who represented the military's interests in the Politburo. Romanov and Grishin were his rivals for the succession after Chernenko.

Second, Gorbachev was only too aware of the possibility that the Polish scenario of a military dictatorship might develop out of the turmoil of perestroika. Indeed, had it not been for Gorbachev's moves to neutralize the army in advance, he might have become the last civilian leader of the Soviet Union. The logical alternative under the circumstances was to become the last Soviet leader altogether. However, there is no reason to think that such an alternative occurred to him at the time.

Perhaps the most momentous consequences came from the new public image of the army created in the media. Criticism was triggered by showing to the Congress of People's Deputies a videotape from the Georgian capital, Tbilisi, where the army used poison gas against civilians. This antimilitary show was televised across the country—the first nationwide transmission of the proceedings of the congress ordered by Gorbachev.

Turnover among the military leadership under Gorbachev rivals only "that resulting from Stalin's bloody purge of 1937."[54] William Odom called this rapid turnover a "revitalization of cadres." On closer examination, however, such an opinion is difficult to sustain. As in 1937–38, the purges of 1987–88 resulted in a decapitated army rather than a revitalized one. Unlike the massive personnel changes in the party apparatus, those in the army did not bring to its highest posts a new, better-educated generation. On the contrary, the new military appointments meant that able generals with well-established professional reputations and high authority within the officer corps were replaced by older, third-rate staff brought from the Asian military districts.

The Mathias Rust affair, the landing of a small Cessna plane on Red Square by a German youth in March 1987, gave Gorbachev an excuse for a thorough purge in the air forces, the most professional elite in the Soviet army. At that time, General Dmitri Yazov was appointed defense minister. Yazov was a particularly undistinguished figure in the Soviet military establishment, which had already been seriously weakened by Andropov. That Yazov had been prepared for taking over the Ministry of Defense in advance of the Rust affair was clear; several months earlier he had been called from his Central Asian Military District to Moscow and given a "waiting job" as head of the ministry's personnel department. The last Soviet marshal, Sergei Akhromeyev, resigned to head the general staff shortly after Gorbachev announced unilateral reductions in the Soviet armed forces in his speech to the United Nations in December 1988. An obscure officer, Colonel General Moiseyev, became the new chief of the general staff, which was an "insult to the tradition of the post."[55]

As a result of such unorthodox personnel policy, the army received a leadership with little authority over its own ranks, as the August coup clearly showed. Before that happened, personnel changes were soon followed by tinkering with defense structures. This approach began in 1989 with Gorbachev's disclosure of the composition of the Defense Council, the supreme organ for defense coordination. The American analyst William Odom concluded that the Defense Council would become more central in future defense policy making. In fact, Gorbachev made the disclosure about the Defense Council only as a means to severely criticize it. In the council's disclosed membership, no KGB representative was mentioned, which in itself indicated its decreased importance. As Odom pointed out, the Defense Council "suffered an eclipse" with the creation of the Presidential Council, which included most of its members. The law on the Presidential Council altogether omitted any role for the Defense Council.

Another body to eclipse the Defense Council was the newly created Committee of the Supreme Soviet for Defense and State Security. This committee aspired to legislate on the powers of the Defense Council, although its powers were largely fictitious considering its members' lack of experience in military matters. In any case, the Supreme Soviet Committee would not have been allowed to meddle with the Defense Council had the council retained its usual power after Gorbachev's presidential reform. At the same time, the size of the general staff was reduced by 20 percent and its powers trimmed.

A further sign of the decreased military standing was the removal of all border troops, MVD forces, and KGB formations from military command. This move was reversed in late 1991, when Gorbachev finally realized that he had lost control over the country. The charismatic general of the air forces, Boris Gromov, was put in command of all paramilitary formations with the task of preparing them for domestic emergencies. According to the same plan, the "nationality question" was to be dealt with, among other means, by the abolition of the fifteen Soviet republics and their replacement by forty to sixty meta-ethnic units.[56]

But that was already too late. In the disarray of perestroika, neither the capacity nor the structures were left to take control of the country. The only force that could have done it was the army. By that time, however, the military was sulking, its leadership had little authority and competence, and its most able officers had been demoted. General Yazov was a convenient military leader for the time of peace, but his efforts in an emergency to mobilize the officer corps failed.

In this way, the KGB found itself victorious among the ruins of the empire, albeit ruins which were of its own making.

Chapter 4

The Miracle of

German Unification

Here now, gentlemen, whatever we manage to get into the barn will
be safe. — Chancellor Helmut Kohl instructing his team on the way to
Moscow in July 1990

When asked by David Pryce-Jones why the Soviet Union, after so
many years of massive military buildup, gave up its Western front
for practically nothing in return, the last head of the CC International Department, Valentin Falin, said: "We are still waiting for
the answer to that from Gorbachev. . . . He confided in no one.
He spoke on the phone directly to Kohl."[1]

Many observers agree that Gorbachev's foreign policy led to
the fall of the Berlin Wall and the subsequent dissolution of the
Warsaw Pact. Never before had an empire made such profound
voluntary concessions to parties considered inimical in its traditional security doctrine—in this case Germany and the United
States. The evolution of Soviet foreign policy, from alternatives
that in 1983 still included the possibility of a first nuclear strike
to a completely different worldview reflected in the New Thinking, is yet to be explained. What follows is not a blow-by-blow
description of the New Thinking, but a discussion of its turning
point, sometimes called the miracle of German unification.

The unification of the two Germanies has been the most important event shaping international relations in the second half of
the twentieth century. The Soviet Union's dissolution can be considered its most immediate geopolitical consequence; the Soviet
loss of key strategic position in Europe triggered the process of
territorial retrenchment, pushing the range of Moscow's domina-

tion back to the East. The process is continuing and reaches well beyond the Continent as a series of geopolitical aftershocks follows a major earthquake. Such momentous consequences rarely can be traced back to a single decision made by one man. Yet the reasons why Gorbachev acquiesced in German unification on terms so favorable for the Western Allies are anything but clear.

In this chapter the existing explanations of why Gorbachev made such wide concessions to Chancellor Helmut Kohl will be carefully examined—and shown wanting—because they miss some important circumstances under which the decisions were made by the Soviet leader. A new interpretation of these events is offered, based on the personal and ideological considerations discussed in chapter 1.

The Caucasian Meeting

It is a hot Sunday, 15 July 1990. Gorbachev and Kohl, with their staffs, are boarding a large helicopter in Stavropol, which will take them to a hunting lodge in the Caucasus. The German chancellor's visit is a working summit to settle the final terms of German unification. Kohl has already scored two important points. At the meeting in Moscow the day before, Gorbachev unequivocally accepted NATO membership of a united Germany. This was the first such unambiguous statement after several months of mixed signals from Moscow. The second point concerned the status of the soon-to-be united Germany; Gorbachev acquiesced in lifting the rights of the Four Powers on German territory *immediately* upon unification.

These were extraordinarily good terms for Kohl. Ending the status of occupation by the Four Powers was negotiated in a series of Two-Plus-Four meetings. Had the Soviet Union insisted, negotiations concerning the internal process of German unification could have been separated from the Two-Plus-Four Agreement. What is more, Gorbachev would have received tacit support on this issue from France, Britain, and Italy—not to mention other countries, such as Poland, all of which felt that their legitimate interests were being disregarded in the super-powers' game. Even the United States, which unreservedly sup-ported German unification, might have been persuaded against the cumulative solution of the German question, considering the unpredictable consequences that such a radical shift in interna-tional relations might evoke.[2] Although Kohl understandably did not like the idea of settling the issue of unification separately from that of sovereignty, he would have had no choice but to accept what was on the table.[3] As it happened, he got both concessions in one swoop.

The remaining points concerned security arrangements dur-ing the transitional period, and they were to be discussed over a glass of vodka at a table set in a Caucasian meadow.[4] This log cabin German-Soviet diplomacy originated one year earlier when the Gorbachevs visited the Kohls in their bungalow in Bonn, and both couples agreed to visit each other's native places—or this was how Gorbachev explained the unusual circumstances in which decisions on a new world order were to be made.

Further Soviet concessions came to the Germans almost effort-lessly. First, Soviet troops would withdraw from East Germany within four years. Although the NATO structures themselves would not be extended until the Soviet troops had withdrawn completely, NATO security guarantees would immediately apply to the East German territory. Also, Bundeswehr units could be stationed in East Germany immediately after unification, provid-ing that they were not integrated with NATO. In return, Ger-many would limit its forces to 370,000 (rather than 350,000, as was originally suggested by the Soviet side) and renounce atomic, biological, and chemical weapons, something the Federal Repub-lic had already pledged to do.

Although the Germans had been confident of a generally posi-tive result from this summit, nobody expected it to be such a tremendous success. On each of the points that he conceded, Gorbachev could have made legitimate reservations, with more or less open support from Britain and France. In the end, the Germans received more than they realistically could have hoped for if Gorbachev had pressed them as hard as he was in a position to do. The point is that he was unwilling to press hard.

When the deal in the Caucasus was sealed, problems arose over prompt communication from such a remote location to Washington, D.C. The first news reached U.S. Secretary of State James Baker and his staff only the following day, on their arrival in Paris for the Two-Plus-Four meeting.[5] Reporters noticed the surprise of U.S. officials and quickly concluded that the Germans had struck a deal with the Russians while leaving Washington in the dark.

The impression was wrong: "The Germans had done precisely what they told the [U.S.] president they would do," Philip Zelikov and Condolenza Rice tell us in their account of American diplomacy surrounding the process of German unification.[6] They make a persuasive case that without sustained U.S. diplomacy in the period preceding the Caucasus deal, the German achievement would have been highly unlikely. To take just one example, only the United States was able to sway the reluctant NATO allies into signing the London declaration on radical changes in defense strategy. In the London declaration the Western Allies renounced their enmity toward the Soviet Union; the strategy of forward defense and flexible response was effectively consigned to the past. This, in turn, made it possible for Gorbachev to accept a united Germany's membership in NATO.

The account by Zelikov and Rice makes the process appear to be a concert of well-informed, coordinated, and timely actions. If the German chancellor is to be credited in seizing the opportunity when it occurred, so is the American president. The U.S. government's strategic purpose, however, unlike that of Germany, does not seem entirely clear. An objective such as retaining a united Germany within NATO does not need further justification. But U.S. endeavors aimed to do more than simply preserve the status quo; such a limited goal would not have been realistic, anyhow. What may puzzle observers is how scant attention was given in the midst of such fierce activity to the larger picture of what would happen next. Admittedly, such consequences as the dissolution of the Soviet Union did not figure on the American agenda. It was as if the United States won the cold war by accident, in the course of helping the Germans to unite.

The American account reveals several episodes of misunderstanding across the Atlantic, illustrating archetypal differences in political thinking. For example, Zelikov and Rice present us with the exact date when the cold war ended: on 30 May 1990, during Gorbachev's visit to Washington.[7] At an afternoon meeting in the White House, the subject was a united Germany's future affiliations. President George Bush argued that under the Helsinki principles all nations had the right to choose their own alliances. From this premise it followed that Germany, too, should have the right to decide for itself which alliance it would join. Gorbachev agreed.

The Americans were startled: "They could see Akhromeyev [the Soviet marshal] and Falin [the Politburo's expert on Germany] . . . shifting in their seats. Blackwill [of the U.S. Security Council] jotted down a quick note pointing out to President Bush that, surprisingly, Gorbachev had just supported the U.S. position that nations have the right to choose their own alliances. Could the president get Gorbachev to say it again? Bush could." While Gorbachev was saying it again, there was a commotion among the Soviet delegation, "almost physically distancing themselves from their leader's words." Losing confidence, Gorbachev asked Falin to explain why the Soviets considered a pro-NATO solution for Germany unacceptable. "As Falin launched into his presentation, Gorbachev conferred with Shevardnadze," trying to pass the German issue on to him. "Shevardnadze openly refused, right in front of the Americans saying that the matter had to be decided by heads of government."[8]

Yet it was not the palpable mess within the Soviet delegation that made Zelikov and Rice point to the meeting as fateful. More important for them was Gorbachev's revealed adherence to the principle that nations have the right to choose their own alliances. Bush immediately reported the breakthrough to his European allies Helmut Kohl, Margaret Thatcher, and François Mitterrand (in that order) and was somewhat disappointed by their lack of enthusiasm. Why, Gorbachev had just said that nations have the right. . . . But Kohl was more preoccupied with economic issues; would the United States be willing to provide economic aid to the Soviet Union? Thatcher was also unimpressed, whereas Mitterrand remarked shrewdly that Gorbachev might be hoping to achieve his security objectives through West Germany's domestic politics (peace movements and the like).[9]

Surprisingly, both the American idealists and the European skeptics got it right. Gorbachev's beliefs were important for the way in which the cold war ended. But neither the Soviet establishment nor the Soviet public could live with the consequences of their leader's ideas for very much longer. What, then, were Gorbachev's ideas?

The "Why" Question

Analyses of the politics of German unification are plentiful, and, although a lot more work will have to be done to shed light on all of the backstage dealings, the general picture seems relatively clear. The situation was completely new, complex, and developing very fast, in some cases exceeding the abilities of the statesmen involved. In fact, only the Germans had a clear goal—to unite on the best possible terms. The Americans also were calmly composed, firmly supporting the Germans, whom they had chosen as their major European partner even before the onset of these fateful developments. As Hans-Dietrich Genscher told Timothy Garton Ash, the results were decided between Bonn and Moscow with important input from Washington. Genscher called this arrangement "two and a half" as opposed to the official Two-Plus-Four formula.[10]

In the final reckoning, everything hinged on Gorbachev. Yet explanations of why he was so forthcoming with regard to the German objectives have been far from satisfactory. Many commentators at the time, especially German and American analysts, pointed out that it was wiser for the Soviets to accept NATO membership for a united Germany than to leave it as a loose cannon on the European deck. This is a good example of the West projecting its own interests onto the Soviet perspective. When confronted with this argument, the old hand of Soviet foreign policy, Valentin Falin, replied, "Don't treat us like kids." [11] In fact, Gorbachev's concessions to the Western Allies meant for the Soviet Union a loss of its sphere of influence over a substantial part of Europe and a major setback in terms of its international position as a superpower.

An analyst of German unification may be prone to at least two biases. First of all, an appealing aura surrounded the German developments, which swayed popular opinion in favor of Germany, perhaps for the first time since World War II. Thus, liberals and nationalists alike have perceived German unification as the right thing to do; the same is true of ordinary people with no particular predispositions. A theory that the right cause has won because it was right is strongly compelling.

Second, when there is a need to explain political decisions with important consequences but no obvious reasons to support them, a temptation exists to make up such reasons by retrospective rationalizing. In this instance it has led to the conclusion that Gorbachev had little choice but to do what he did because (1) he needed Western economic assistance, (2) his political situation at home was deteriorating, and (3) communism was collapsing all over East-Central Europe, which made it impossible for the Soviet Union to cling to its outer empire for much longer. Let us take up each of these issues separately and see how they relate to Gorbachev's German policy.

The Great Buy

The economic motive for Gorbachev's German policy is sometimes overemphasized. For example, Kohl's adviser at the time of unification, Horst Teltschik, claims that the Soviet Union was then "close to economic collapse" because of its inability to repay its debts, which is an obvious exaggeration.[12] True, in the turmoil of perestroika, especially in the critical period 1989–90, the Soviet leadership had serious problems servicing its current debts as well as maintaining domestic supplies, and Kohl was extremely generous in providing timely aid. Trainloads of foodstuffs were dispatched to the USSR throughout the negotiations, and a cheap credit of DM 5 billion was quickly arranged on the understanding that it was just part of what Germany was prepared to pay.[13] A further DM 12 billion in aid and a DM 3 billion credit for resettling Soviet troops at home were agreed to within a month of the Caucasus meeting.[14]

However, even if all the German payments, totaling as much as DM 60 billion,[15] are taken into consideration, one does not trade the key strategic positions of an empire for such sums. Further, the way in which Gorbachev was making his financial requests, that is, raising them weeks after the agreement was signed, indicates that he was trying to make the most of a decision that had been taken for markedly different reasons.

If direct German payments cannot fully explain Gorbachev's goodwill, another economic perspective has been considered as a possible motive for his concessions—the new cooperative relationship with the West that would permit modernization of the Soviet Union. But the Soviet leadership already had enjoyed a "new cooperative relationship" with the West for at least three years, and this relationship did not and could not bring much in the way of improvement without a firm commitment to economic reforms. Such reforms, however, were not on the Gorbachev agenda. Ever since party reformers, led by Boris Yeltsin, walked out of the Twenty-Eighth Party Congress right before Kohl's visit, Gorbachev had been perfectly aware that perestroika was coming to a halt.

The price that Gorbachev paid for his reelection as general secretary was restoration of the conservative party apparatus to its previous position of power (see chapter 2). In the following months (autumn of 1990) Gorbachev would desert his radical advisers in favor of more traditional apparatchiks, with whom he would try to wind up perestroika rather than expand it with a package of economic reforms. This intention was confirmed by yet another five-year plan presented at the time by his prime minister, Nikolai Ryzhkov. As far as market reforms were concerned, they were not on Gorbachev's agenda but on that of his democratic opposition, headed by Yeltsin. Clever operator in party politics that he was, Gorbachev must have known as much when he received Kohl in the Caucasus.

In fact, economic considerations do not seem to have been paramount for Gorbachev when he was making up his mind on the German question. Even Teltschik, who first advanced the economic thesis to explain the German success in the Caucasus, finally had to admit that the economic arguments merely helped "to save the face both of the Soviet Union and Gorbachev."[16] However, such arguments could scarcely serve this purpose, since Gorbachev was promptly accused by his own apparatus of selling out East Germany. Teltschik seemed at a loss when confronted with this dilemma: "Sure, but what was the alternative?"—he meant the alternative for the German side—"We were aware we had to do something, and that meant paying for reunification."[17] This could be yet another version of "cheque-book diplomacy," a reflex response of German statesmen to political problems, as described by Timothy Garton Ash.[18]

In this case, however, the perplexed Germans were paying for something that they knew money alone could not buy. While preparing a package to help Gorbachev get over the hurdle with his own apparatus, Kohl's advisers were in fact providing the Soviet leader with an excuse to do what he already seemed determined to do. The package they put together, including the bilateral German-Soviet treaty on cooperation and the London declaration about changing NATO's policy, was nothing more than it was meant to be—an excuse.

Domestic Imperatives

Another set of explanations for Gorbachev's German policy points to the political crisis in the Soviet Union at that time. Thus, the New Thinking was, as Ash put it, "a classic example of what in German historiography has been called the *Primat der Innenpolitik,* the primacy of domestic political imperatives."[19] Such a direct transfer of policy concepts from Germany to the Soviet Union could in itself be the cause of possible misunderstanding.

It would be plausible to explain such policies as the withdrawal from Afghanistan, or the signing of the Geneva treaty (on the reduction of intermediate-range nuclear forces), by domestic considerations, either economic (curbing military spending) or political (boosting perestroika). But Gorbachev persisted in his New Thinking even after he had given up his domestic reforms. As perestroika had crumbled at home, making him switch alliances back and forth between democrats and hard-liners, the New Thinking was growing in range and scope, from the Bonn Declaration of June 1989 (on not interfering with the internal affairs of Soviet satellites) to the terms of German unification accepted by Gorbachev in the summer of 1990.

Indeed, it might be argued that ever since his United Nations speech in December 1988, Gorbachev had been trying to shape his domestic circumstances in such a way as to secure for himself maximum freedom in foreign policy choices. In this effort, he largely succeeded. In the period following the Twenty-Eighth Party Congress, when Gorbachev was making crucial decisions on German unification, he was at the peak of his power at home. Yeltsin had walked out of the party session, but his strength as leader of the democratic opposition had not yet been consolidated. And Gorbachev's main conservative opponent, Yegor Ligachev, was out of the game. The military had been neutralized back in 1988 after a German youth's landing of a Cessna in Red Square gave Gorbachev an excuse for extensive purges (see chapter 3).

Thus, at the time of Gorbachev's Caucasian deal, his position at home was practically unchallenged. This was confirmed by the Central Committee's prompt ratification of his decisions, despite the International Department's misgivings.[20] That much Ash has noted as well. The conundrum of Gorbachev's German policy can best be appreciated when we see that even the most clear-minded analyst gets caught in the trap of retrospective rationalization along the lines of "he did it because he had to do it." But the opposite interpretation may be closer to the truth—that is, Gorbachev made the deal with Kohl not because he had to do it but because he was free to do it.

Had Gorbachev made up his mind about the German question in response to his domestic problems, he never would have gone beyond trading German unification for German neutrality, an option already tried on the Germans by Stalin back in 1952. This time around the Germans would have been pressed much harder to reconsider that option. (Zelikov and Rice offer some evidence that such a reconsideration was in fact taking place.)[21] Any more concessions—concessions to Kohl, in particular—were bound to worsen rather than solve Gorbachev's domestic problems, as they would necessarily imply the loss of East-Central Europe.

In the first place, Gorbachev's concessions to the Germans aggravated the nationalities problem in the Soviet Union, making it even more intractable; the Balts followed the Poles, Hungarians, and Czechs in turning their first parliamentary elections into a plebiscite on Soviet domination. Second, Gorbachev's unorthodox policy toward Eastern Europe alienated the military even further, thus making him still more vulnerable in the forthcoming confrontation with Yeltsin. As his last foreign minister, Alexander Besmertnyk, said: "After the unification of Germany [Gorbachev] had crossed a critical line as far as the Soviet public was concerned . . . . The army and the older generation which had gone through the war were angered."[22]

That still leaves us with the initial question: Why did Gorbachev give up East Central Europe? The argument that the "outer" empire was already lost because popular rebellions swept satellite communist parties from power needs to be treated separately in a wider context.

Switching Tracks

New directions in Soviet foreign policy were adopted by the Twenty-Third Soviet Party Conference and proclaimed in Gorbachev's UN speech in December 1988. The most important proposal was Gorbachev's advocacy of common human values, which was tantamount to renouncing class struggle as the leading strategy for dealing with the West. Skeptics questioned the degree of difference between the approach of common human values and the traditional approach of peaceful coexistence, which never had prevented the Soviet Union from pursuing its expansionist second track. There was a significant difference, however. Although the dual-track policy was still in place (the Soviet Union was to remain the champion of socialism, albeit with a human face), the foundations of both tracks shifted. The track that was originally ideological, that is, the expansion of socialism, became merely pragmatic, whereas the one that was initially pragmatic, peaceful coexistence, became infused with ideology and messianism.

In other words, relations with the West received the positive ideological load previously attached to the objective of its destruction. At the same time, relations with the socialist world lost their former preponderance; those relations that continued were to be based on the principle of free choice. The ideological conversion of the Soviet leadership was confirmed by such concessions as unilateral reductions in Soviet troops and the withdrawal of five thousand tanks from Eastern Europe, with a commitment toward complete withdrawal in the future. Thus, signals were sent to satellite parties that they should find their own power base at home instead of relying on traditional "fraternal" help. In response, the Polish communists invited Lech Wałęsa to Round Table talks, the Hungarians got rid of the aging János Kádár and formed a new government for reform, while Czechoslovak and East German communists simply banned Soviet newspapers from entering their countries.

When asked by Polish intellectuals in Warsaw whether the principle of free choice meant the end of the Brezhnev Doctrine, Gorbachev's answer was angry and negative.[23] In fact, then, the new principle was clearly for Western consumption, whereas those directly concerned were to be offered the choice of reformed socialism. The New Thinking was about Westpolitik, designed to provide the Soviet Union and its leader with legitimacy in relations with the Western world.

At this stage Gorbachev clearly believed in the possibility that the Warsaw Pact could be converted into something like NATO— a friendly union of states with common interests, run by reformed communist parties vested with a popular mandate. What he miscalculated was the possibility that such reforms might have materialized without the Soviet Union's direct involvement. The ultimate reliance on Soviet might was the linchpin of the unwritten constitutions in all of the Soviet satellite countries. Once this vital element was gone, each structure was shaken to its foundation regardless of whether the ruling elite remained orthodox or was replaced by reform-minded apparatchiks. In each case the governing party split apart and lost its ability to govern.

To be sure, various groups and factions had always been present within satellite parties, but Moscow had been the highest arbiter on which group was right, which group was wrong, and what the party line should be.[24] As soon as Gorbachev gave up this right of arbitration, the fraternal parties were left with no clear mechanism to reach a consensus. "Reformers and hard-liners were cutting the ground away from under each other's feet by mutual discreditation,"[25] David Pryce-Jones asserted. As the communist parties disintegrated, so did the regimes over which they presided, since no other structures were in place to take up government functions.

The Tautology of East European Revolutions

A growing number of interviews and memoirs of political actors from those years show that the explanation of Gorbachev's German policy by reference to the dramatic developments in Eastern Europe in 1989 may be merely a tautology; the East European revolutions were not the cause but the outcome of Gorbachev's insistence on not interfering in the satellites' domestic affairs. The case of Poland, where the Solidarity movement of 10 million strong emerged even under the Brezhnev regime, was an exception rather than the rule.

But in the end, Poland also fell into the general pattern; by 1988, the Jaruzelski regime was economically unsuccessful, but it was not collapsing either. The crucial decision to invite Solidarity to the Round Table was made only in the second half of 1988 by party leaders who took their cue from the Twenty-Third Soviet Party Conference. A parallel option, suggested at the time by Prime Minister Mieczysław Rakowski, was the Chinese solution—that is, the market economy without democracy. For this to work, however, the party needed Moscow's continuous involvement in Polish affairs, and in the absence of such involvement, the Rakowski government had little chance to pursue any alternative course of action than Round Table talks with its opponents.

Solidarity leaders kept bringing Soviet newspapers to their meetings with the government as the best arguments for their cause.[26] As a seasoned party apparatchik confessed to an opposition leader during the Round Table talks:

We really don't know what Russian intentions are any more. All our contacts have snapped. Until recently, we were contacting a group of people whom we knew well. They understood our interests and we understood theirs. Now everything has changed. They are pragmatic and we don't have access to them any more.[27]

The New Thinking considerably influenced the speed and direction of developments in Poland. Even after winning the June

1989 elections, Solidarity leaders were vulnerable to Soviet pressure, as can be seen from the 19 August 1989 episode. On that day, when Tadeusz Mazowiecki received the mandate to form his government, the Polish ambassador in Bucharest, as well as all other Warsaw Pact ambassadors, received a letter from the Romanian government harshly criticizing developments in Poland in language reminiscent of the 1956 and 1968 Soviet invasions. The letter inspired horror among Solidarity leaders; everyone waited to see how Gorbachev would respond. Only when Gorbachev refused to receive the Romanian ambassador in Moscow did Mazowiecki go ahead to form the first Solidarity government.[28]

The Hungarian Decision

The decision to dismantle controls on the Austrian border, which let East Germans flood to the West, was taken by the reformed but still communist Hungarian government without its consulting with Moscow. The absence of such talks, however, stemmed not from Hungarian unwillingness to talk but from Moscow's relative indifference to the subject. When the Soviet ambassador in Budapest received suggestions that the new prime minister, Miklos Nemeth, should meet Gorbachev, Moscow displayed little interest. The Soviet leadership obviously knew about the Hungarian government's plans to dismantle border controls, since those plans were made with the participation of the Hungarian ministers of interior and defense, both of whom at the time were closely connected to their Soviet counterparts. "The KGB chief [in Budapest] never came to me about the opening of the border," the interior official related. "But I know for a fact that the KGB did not think it would be of such consequence."[29]

Dismantling controls was one thing, but the treatment of East Germans crossing the border was another. The earlier practice, whereby a German captured in Hungary while trying to cross the Austrian border was transferred back to East Germany, was suspended in July 1989. Soon afterward, East Germans began to gather in Hungary. They did not try to cross into Austria, but they camped in parks and waited. When in mid-August their numbers approached 40,000, it was clear that something had to be done, especially since their presence in the West German embassies in Budapest and Prague was creating a scandal.

Consultations proceeded between Budapest and Berlin, but *Moscow expressed no interest* in solving the problem one way or the other. Budapest followed Moscow's line—the Honecker government was made to understand that Hungary "was not going to be their gendarme any more."[30] The two German governments were asked to settle the issue between themselves. The Bonn government sent requests to Budapest to treat the migrants as West German citizens, but the Hungarians asked Bonn to negotiate with Berlin.

A stalemate followed, and the foreign minister, Gyula Horn, went to Berlin to give his East German comrades a deadline for solving the problem. When the first deadline expired, another was given on 11 September, and only after that was the West German solution adopted.[31] Before that happened, however, the Hungarian government managed to cash in DM 1 billion on the new policy as a token of gratitude from Chancellor Kohl.[32] Yet Prime Minister Nemeth was "constantly testing how far [the Hungarians] could go . . . because they were unsure what finally Gorbachev might do, and could only discover this by experience."[33] Thus, Soviet indifference encouraged the developments in Poland and Hungary rather than the opposite.

The East German Chaos

Perhaps the clearest case of the disintegration of a communist regime prompted by the removal of its linchpin, Soviet responsibility, was what happened in East Germany in 1989. The East German case was especially dramatic since it involved the disruption not only of the regime but also of society, which had had few other bonds to keep it together. The picture emerging from

a series of interviews conducted by David Pryce-Jones shows
clearly that what Germans have called their "revolution" was
simply the progressive disintegration of the East German governing party, resulting directly from Gorbachev's lack of a policy
toward Soviet satellites.[34]

During the crucial period the East German machinery of coercion was still intact, but it received no orders since no one was
in a position to give them. The Berlin Wall itself opened through
sheer chaos. The local Berlin apparatchik, Günter Schabowski,
possibly when inebriated, said something ambiguous on the matter to the press, which brought its own interpretation of the news
to West German TV, where it was immediately broadcast.[35] A
short time later, the Bundestag in Bonn rose to sing the national
anthem, and East Berliners were crowding Checkpoint Charlie.

Since East German border guards had no clear instructions on
what to do with the crowd, they did as they pleased, which meant
letting people go.[36] While people were flooding through Checkpoint Charlie, a few hundred meters away at Brandenburger Tor
the border guards stood shoulder to shoulder, and water cannons
were deployed to scare people off. "It was incomprehensible to see
the border guards there as meanwhile people were crossing the
border everywhere else," an East German military commander
said. "Five hundred yards away on the Potsdamer Platz they were
going and coming as they liked. . . . It made no sense."[37]

The extent of the chaos became clear to the commander of
the East Berlin military district, Colonel Jürgen Sürkau, when he
came to the meeting summoned that same night by the minister
of defense, Kessler. The minister opened the meeting by saying
that the party was losing public confidence.

All hell broke loose. I was shocked . . . others shouted to Kessler . . . to
sit down. One colonel actually ordered the Minister to stop. . . . General
Baumgarten [in charge of border guards] stood up to say, "Comrades,
we are facing the outbreak of war". . . . The commander of the First
Mechanized Division told Baumgarten not to play with our patriotic
feelings, as he could detect no danger of war. He said, "You have not
understood that the game is over, but it is, there is no war, everything is

over and done with. . . ." This meeting never came to an orderly conclusion as more and more officers began pulling out of their pockets letters [of] resignation. . . . It was such a shock for a soldier to realise that the army was in effect leaderless.[38]

Colonel Sürkau, who described himself as a communist until the very end, decided to speak directly to the West German Bundeswehr. He crossed over to West Berlin, looked up addresses in the telephone book, and got in touch with the right people. More meetings ensued on both sides of the border "to ensure that from the army's point of view nothing went wrong."[39]

Common Human Values and the Question of Strategy

From this point on, Gorbachev's choice was between using Soviet troops stationed in East Germany or giving up Eastern Europe altogether. In December 1989 his spokesman officially repudiated the Brezhnev Doctrine at a press conference in Washington, D.C., and presented the Sinatra doctrine instead: everyone does it his way. In the spring of 1990 the possibility still existed that Soviet leaders could use the 364,000 troops stationed in East Germany to maintain the division of the two Germanies or at least to influence the Two-Plus-Four talks already under way. This action could have been justified in the name of international law since the Soviet Union had occupation rights in East Germany, according to the Four-Power Agreement still in force. This was what experts in the CC International Department urged Gorbachev to do.[40] A careful analysis led Hannes Adomeit to conclude: "The Soviet leadership rejected this course of action, to repeat, not because it was forced to do so, but because of its firm commitment to a comprehensive withdrawal of Soviet forces from Central Europe and its determination to come to a modus vivendi with Germany."[41]

Adomeit does not explain, however, why this modus vivendi had to be so favorable to the Germans or why Gorbachev was so determined to withdraw Soviet forces from Central Europe in the first place, especially since the initial scenario of "reformed communism" had already failed. The most interesting feature of the Caucasian deal was that, at the time it was made, its consequences were already clear. In the first democratic elections held throughout Eastern Europe, communist governments, reformed or otherwise, were sent packing. This change also had a powerful impact on parliamentary elections held soon afterward in the Soviet republics, especially in the Baltics and Caucasus.

This was the political context in which Gorbachev made his decisions about Germany. Clearly, his decision to withdraw Soviet forces rather than use them was out of the ordinary, if Soviet or, indeed, Russian traditions are considered. So what stopped Gorbachev from doing what his predecessors would not have hesitated to do? No simple answer can be found to this question, but some circumstances preceding and parallel to Gorbachev's decision may add to our understanding.

The freedom of choice enjoyed by Gorbachev in making foreign policy at that particular time is one such unusual circumstance. It has been argued that, contrary to popular opinion that "he had to do it," Gorbachev had more room to make his own decisions in foreign policy than any other Soviet leader except Stalin. The methods that he applied to achieve this degree of independence also resembled Stalin's. Except for terror, all of the Stalinist tools were used in perestroika. The purges in the party apparatus were bloodless, but just as massive, and the same is true for the purges in the military; both Stalin and Gorbachev downgraded the party, supplanting it by various councils and committees piled one on another with no clearly defined powers.

A certain similarity can be found between Stalin's surprise at Hitler's invasion and Gorbachev's bewilderment at the loss of his empire. In both cases all the necessary information and advice were at hand, but the experts were locked out of the most important decisions. Of course, there were more differences than similarities between Stalin and Gorbachev that led to the differences in their respective achievements. Perhaps the most important contrast was Gorbachev's hatred of bloodshed. As his collaborators agreed, he was a man of peace. Such men do not make efficient despots.

The role of the military in Gorbachev's German policy was conspicuous for its absence. The determination with which he put down his own military has been discussed in chapter 3. This went well beyond the logic of departmental competition that he inherited from his late patron and KGB chair, Yuri Andropov. Purges in the military reached their height in the spring of 1987 when the elite air forces were cleansed in the aftermath of the Rust affair and the new defense minister, General Dmitri Yazov, was appointed. The last redneck, Marshal Sergei Akhromeyev, resigned from the Soviet Military Command on the very day that Gorbachev delivered his 1988 speech to the United Nations.

Gorbachev made the military establishment completely loyal to him, but he risked the chance that, should an emergency arise, the military would be ineffective. The purged generals, who also were the ablest, enjoyed high standing with the officer corps. Neither General Yazov nor the new chief of staff, Marshal M. Moiseyev, commanded the same authority in the armed forces as their predecessors. Gorbachev would have had to eat humble pie if he wanted a reconciliation with the army. What is more, at the time in question (the first half of 1990), the most outspoken military leader, General Nikolai Ogarkov, was the commander of the Soviet forces stationed on the German-Polish border (with their headquarters in Legnica). Had those forces been activated, Ogarkov would have returned to his previous political prominence. The entire effort made to harness the military, which was one of the key objectives of perestroika, would have been wasted.

Still more important, once the military had recovered its political influence, it would have been likely to take over the political stage altogether; in the turmoil of perestroika, the Polish scenario must have been Gorbachev's worst nightmare. With the benefit of hindsight we now can see that a military or semimilitary regime was the only way to prevent the rapid disintegration of the Soviet Union at that time. Evidence abounds that Gorbachev did not consider such an alternative as a possible outcome of his policy.

Gorbachev did not have a policy toward East Central Europe; he took his empire for granted. The principle of free choice was introduced into the Warsaw Pact not to dissolve it but to make it more like NATO. As Valentin Falin, Gorbachev's best expert on Germany, put it: "He did not understand how it really was; he thought it might be possible to keep relations between [the two German] states frozen while trying to normalize them."

A similar confusion was evident in the conduct of the Soviet foreign minister. After delivering a tough speech to the United Nations in September 1989, warning the Germans against defying postwar realities, Eduard Shevardnadze discussed with the Hungarian prime minister, Gyula Horn, the problem of German refugees. Shevardnadze's opinion was that those people "should just be allowed to go because they could not be stopped by force." The Soviet foreign minister did not seem to see any inconsistency between his resignation to the GDR's circumstances and the warning speech he had just delivered that "postwar realities" could not be revised.[42]

Postmodern Ideas and Imperial Hubris

Gorbachev tried to secure his place in the club of the Western powers by means of postmodern logic. He dismissed the cold war division into friends and enemies as if it were no more than an accident of faulty communication without real content or significance. But the world refuses to change so easily. While Gorbachev was trying to improve Soviet "communication" with the West, Kohl instructed his team on its way to Moscow: "here now, gentlemen, whatever we manage to get into the barn will be safe."[43]

The same postmodern logic did away with Soviet military doctrine. The principle of class struggle, which justified previous Soviet aggression, was replaced by common human values. The Soviet Union's messianic mission was no longer to destroy the capitalist world but to cooperate with it. This is not to argue that the previous Soviet perception of the outside world as an unceasing menace of hostile encirclement had been realistic. It had not been, because the Soviet Union had been under no real threat of military aggression from NATO. The traditional pessimistic perspective made it possible, however, to at least identify an enemy, which was a precondition for having a defense doctrine in the first place—a dilemma well known to NATO today.

Ironically, the reason why Gorbachev's elite was so easily smitten by postmodern ideas was that those ideas provided an elegant cover for imperial hubris. Contrary to the benign message of the postmodern transformation, in an unstructured "global" and "interdependent" world, the sheer weight of a superpower is greater than in a world driven by a balance of national interests and alliances.

Here was yet another aspect of the deal that Gorbachev hoped he was making with Kohl in the Caucasus: a "special relationship" with Germany. This sort of thing was initiated by Frederick the Great as the principal means to expand his realm, and it later was cultivated by Bismarck to keep that domain secure. In this tradition, Germany and Russia had common imperial interests in defending and, indeed, extending their possessions in Central Europe, and both empires were best off vis-à-vis other European powers when they supported each other. Needless to say, the two most recent examples of this tradition at work, the Rapallo Treaty of 1922 and the Ribbentrop-Molotov pact of 1939, were never mentioned in the negotiations. Nevertheless, the historic ties between Germany and Russia were a recurrent theme during the talks, skillfully played up by Kohl from the moment he noticed how much interest this inspired among the Soviet negotiators.[44]

In this context, the bilateral treaty of German-Soviet cooperation was very important for Gorbachev. It is only in this context that the vague treaty statements on the history of mutual relations can be understood—a history that should be completely erased but at the same time continued.[45] However, the political substance of the treaty itself was vague. For example, it stated a firm commitment to nonaggression by both parties and called on other states to join this commitment, but it provided neither concrete guarantees nor a legal basis to act on in the case of a crisis. Certainly, such a treaty could not reduce German obligations within NATO, a fact that Gorbachev failed to grasp.

A brilliant tactician in squabbles within the party, Gorbachev was singularly unprepared for politics outside the party apparatus. Once on top, he operated his domestic machinery of power largely through personal trust and orders, while institutions meant little to him. The same seemed to apply in his conduct of international affairs. Probably Gorbachev's main objective was to maintain the personal recognition of Western leaders, the precondition for which was to renounce aggression. That was what he had promised President George Bush and Chancellor Helmut Kohl.[46] He was as devoted to nonintervention as he was to the causes of his former patrons; it had become a question of personal loyalty.

If world affairs were actually run from an enlarged version of the Kremlin, Gorbachev's loyalty to Kohl and Bush certainly would have paid off. But there is no one big Kremlin to run the world. When the time of need came, and Gorbachev was cornered by both democrats and hard-liners, he tried to get his Western mentors to accept the introduction of emergency measures in the Soviet Union: "He was sitting by the phone, kept asking: 'Mr. President, Mr. Chancellor, will you support me?'"[47] To his amazement, after all he had done for them, they would not.

Chapter 5

Conceptual Revisions

In this chapter the major theories explaining the Soviet regime will be examined against its most striking feature—the dynamics of its collapse. No precedent exists for such a sudden downfall of a regime, and a theory that aspires to explain it can be reasonably expected to deal with this phenomenon. I shall try to show that some of the existing theories can do so if only the original insights of their authors are recovered from decades of oversimplification and outright distortion that resulted from the social science model-making mania. Three broad theories will be considered here: the totalitarian, the bureaucratic, and the most general one of modernization.

How Modern Were Communist Societies?

In a special issue of the *National Interest* entitled "Strange Death of Soviet Communism," Francis Fukuyama reprimanded Sovietologists for developing their own models and methods apart from the paradigms of modern social sciences.[1] Had they been more familiar with modernization theory and the collateral models of political development, he said, students of communist regimes would have had a better chance of understanding what was happening in the Soviet Union. Such phenomena as the diffusion of power from the Soviet center to the party's lower reaches, the growing significance of industrial managers and academics, even the growth of mafias inside and outside the party, all were typical facets of a "proto-civil society." In that respect, Fukuyama claimed, the Soviet Union falls into the same category as other countries that have made a recent transition from an agricultural to a modern industrial economy and have had to cope with the vicissitudes of modernity.

It seems, however, that Fukuyama disregarded a considerable part of the output of Soviet studies during the last fifteen years of the USSR's existence. Since the mid-seventies the mainstream production of Sovietology dwelt precisely on current issues and paradigms of the social sciences. Soviet politics were combed to find evidence of phenomena such as institutionalization, managerialism, the formation of interest groups, etc. Western political scientists were often helped in their efforts by modern-thinking sections of the Soviet establishment, who at that stage were re-assured by finding ills typical of Western modernity in the Soviet Union.

In fact, modernization theory was effectively forcing out the theory of totalitarianism as the flagship model.[2] Since the result was more confusion rather than less, one may think that the major paradigms of the social sciences have been found wanting, or at least have been as deficient as the indigenous models of Soviet studies. Indeed, the opposite argument to Fukuyama's can be made, namely, that the postwar social sciences in general, and modernization theory in particular, have neglected or even distorted to their own peril the experience of communist societies.

Modernization theory is a paradigm rather than a theory of exact content. Indeed, the notion of a paradigm is too narrow for the idea that itself gave birth to the social sciences. Disciplines such as economics and sociology owe their existence to the intellectual discovery of changes taking place in Britain and France at the turn of the eighteenth and nineteenth centuries. The idea of a transition from a traditional to a modern economy, society, and culture soon turned into a powerful ideology with its own impact on both the social sciences and political developments.

In the classic version of the paradigm, the process of modernization was either a byproduct of actions undertaken by rational individuals (the invisible hand of classical economics), or it was directed by transcendental forces beyond individual control (historical dialectics). In either case, the modernizing outcome was not intended, and politics merely adapted to economic and social change. That was roughly how successive stages of Western European development were explained from feudalism to capitalism, from a traditional, rigidly stratified society to a more mobile, modern one, with all the political consequences that followed.

Later on, modernization theorists responded to the demand from belated modernizers in their quest for the beneficial changes already achieved in Western Europe. Thus, subsequent models assumed that economic and social transition to modernity may be planned, directed, and brought about by government. Prescriptions for modernization multiplied in the fifties and sixties when demand was particularly high in the postcolonial world and development models were put on political agendas. Industrialization was the prime item, not only for the sake of economic development, but to facilitate social transition. The rise of an urban proletariat in predominantly peasant societies was seen as a necessary social base for modern development.

The modernizing function of Marxist regimes was taken for granted. After all, industrialization, urbanization, mass education, and the secularization of society, as well as other items of modernity were at the top of their agendas. Indeed, some observers saw the Leninist party as the only practical solution to the problems of belated modernization. That democracy may become a hindrance to, rather than precondition for, late modernization was suggested by several theories. Such problems as the consolidation of a political center, effective administration of its policies, and the maintenance of public order may appear almost intractable in societies embracing mass democracy without modern institutional safeguards already in place. Back in the 1960s Samuel P. Huntington summarized the experience of postcolonial development in unequivocal terms: "the non-Western countries of today can have political modernization or they can have democratic pluralism, but they cannot normally have both."[3] In this context, Huntington pointed to the important role of Leninist parties in developing societies. In his opinion, such parties were capable of absorbing political mobilization and creating modern political institutions at the same time.[4] What latecomers in the arts of modernization need most, Huntington wrote, "is the accumulation and concentration of power, not its dispersion, and it is [from] Moscow and Peking and not Washington that this lesson is to be learned . . . ."[5]

A closer examination of the institutional landscape left behind by communist regimes should have given pause to those who saw communist parties as agents of modernity. If colonial rulers often left behind well-structured machinery of administration and trained personnel for new postcolonial governments, not much in this respect can be found in the communist legacy. Democratic governments in Eastern Europe were often prepared to use whatever structures from the former regime might be helpful in discharging their new responsibilities. They found few such structures.

That came as a surprise. After all, the state apparatus left behind by communist regimes was considered strong or even excessive. The general expectation was that once all-powerful state machinery was made accountable to representative institutions, political transition would be accomplished. It soon appeared, however, that the creation of representative institutions by means of popular elections was an easier task than bringing the executive organs into working shape. Indeed, the lack of modern administrative and economic institutions has been the major brake on the entire process of postcommunist transition.[6]

For example, it was easier to draw up laws on taxation and pass them through newly elected parliaments than to set up a working system of tax collection. The finances of a communist state, especially internal budgeting, were more ostensible than real, since the needs of the state were met by the output of enterprises rather than by taxes in money. In effect, rapid industrialization and urbanization were accomplished under the economy in kind. As in a war economy when money is not an object, the first result was a rapid increase of material output in the sectors chosen by the government. But losses of capital efficiency and flexibility as well as shortages of all items not included among the government's priorities were unavoidable.

Among the numerous consequences of such a concept of modernity, one seems particularly striking. An extensive survey has shown that, even though from two-thirds to three-quarters of Russians and other East Europeans now live in urban areas, most of them grow food for their own consumption. Subsistence food production appears to be a widespread practice among urban households in Eastern Europe and even more so in Russia. "Insofar as a farmer is defined as a person spending at least several hours a day growing food, then 29 percent of residents of Russian cities are farmers," the authors concluded.[7]

The urban food growers in the former Soviet bloc show no particular traits that would distinguish them from the rest of their societies. Multiple regression analysis has shown that such properties as income, education, full-time employment or lack of a job had no significant impact on the practice of growing food for one's own consumption; the sufficient as well as necessary condition was simply access to land. Thus, the basic criterion of a modern economy, namely, that food production is a highly specialized task performed by a narrow group of farmers, is clearly not met in communist societies.[8]

Indeed, as far as institutions go, the communist period resulted in a demodernization in most of the countries concerned. The postcommunist transition has largely consisted in the recovery of precommunist financial and commercial institutions, seen as the lost threads of modernization. In the Czech Republic the prewar Cadastral offices were reinstated only in January 1993 to keep records of landholdings, and these offices had to cope with the consequences of the former regime's practices of granting unrecorded and frequently informal property titles. In Poland, attempts have been made to restore prewar local lending and saving associations, so far without much success. Yeltsin's advisers have been busy studying the Stolypin reform, only to find out that the conditions for its reintroduction have already been lost.

If the forces at work on both sides of the Iron Curtain were essentially similar or equivalent in their modernizing impact, how is one to explain such disparate results? Regrettably, modernization scholarship seems largely impervious to empirical data. I have seen no single attempt to test any of the numerous developmental models derived from theories of modernization against data freely available in the former communist countries. On the contrary, the same old paradigm has been applied again and with renewed vigor, this time to explain the collapse of communist regimes.

The key word has become "civil society." This notion has had diverse antecedents in the history of ideas. In the tradition of the early Enlightenment, civil society is a form of government as opposed to the state of nature, whereas in Hegelian dialectics the adversarial role of civil society in relation to the government (state) is stressed.[9] Most often applied in the modern social sciences is the Tocquevillian notion of civil society as a network of voluntary organizations that protect individuals and their interests against the excessive interference of the state. The Tocquevillian meaning, however, has more in common with the liberal tradition of natural law and civil rights than with the Hegelian apologia of the state.

The idea that a civil society may have existed in the legal vacuum of an arbitrary regime that denied not only civil rights but also private property would have struck both Hegel and de Tocqueville as absurd. Nevertheless, the frequent use of the term by East European dissidents has given it a new place in the history of ideas. In this new context, "civil society" was to become a remedy against the "totalitarian state." The underlying creed was that no amount of state pressure could suppress social initiatives that created independent organizations. Such was the message of Václav Havel's famous essay *The Power of the Powerless* as well as Adam Michnik's *Letters from Prison*, and this credo was well-tuned to the sensibilities of Western observers of both left and right. The Neoconservatives found in the dissident idea of civil society an additional argument for cutting back expansion of the welfare state. The New Left, or "unorthodox Marxists," found the principle stimulating in their search for alternatives to ordinary party politics and a capitalist state.

The new meaning of civil society as an alternative to "ordinary" liberal democracy was particularly appealing to a taste for "antipolitics" typical of dissident culture in Eastern Europe. For example, both Havel and Michnik were trying to prevent the split of the all-embracing revolutionary movements, the Civic Forum and Solidarity, into regular political parties, arguing that party politics with its left-right division was already a thing of the past. Thus, the proponents of "civil society" found themselves opposed to the development of a pluralist society. But pluralism was unavoidable under the new circumstances. The only way to prevent it would be to revert to the methods of the regime that had already collapsed.

A conspicuous adversity exists between the idea of a modern society as presumed and practiced by Marxist and Neomarxist modernizers and the empirical features of developed societies. In the Marxist tradition, social development anticipates a simplification of societal structures leading to the elimination of the most persistent modern division into classes. Accordingly, communist takeovers were typically followed by a civil war that resulted in the destruction of the previous societal structures. Wholesale nationalization completed the process. The uniform content of the mass media further enhanced the appearance of social homogeneity. Communist societies were not class societies in either the Marxist or in the Weberian sense, both of those approaches referring to market and property relations.

Empirical sociology has shown, however, that the more developed a society becomes, the more complex its institutions. "There will be more groups, more classes, more occupations, more structures, more roles—and more conflict."[10] Indeed, the absence of a complete array of classes, statuses, social groupings, etc., has been considered as tantamount to the absence of civil society.[11]

The point of contention, therefore, is whether modern social differentiation had in fact developed under communist regimes despite their ideological commitment and political interest in preventing the expression of group interests. To be sure, preexisting social differentiation could not possibly be eliminated without a trace, nor could the most severe repression and indoctrination eradicate economic transactions outside the official framework of redistribution. A perceptive observer of Ukrainian culture described how the ever-present threat of Mongol intrusions shaped the manners of local trade. Merchants displayed their goods so that they were able to pull up their businesses at the blow of a whistle and disappear into the nearby bushes. The same style of trading returned under Soviet rule.[12]

Moreover, communist leaderships were in the business of government, and government cannot be conducted without a rudimentary organization, delegation of powers, giving some groups better access to goods and privileges, etc.[13] All this organization, in turn, created a certain type of social stratification, various entrenched interests, and countervailing centers to defend them. In particular, the late communist regime was incapable of effectively controlling its own territorial administrations.

All the same, this defective centralization did not translate into pluralism, as some observers of Soviet politics had it. Nor did the growing powers of republican and provincial secretaries spawn the structures of civil society that would eventually bring down the regime. On the contrary, the Soviet barons, Vladimir Shcherbitsky of Ukraine, Dinmuhammed Kunayev of Kazakhstan, Viktor Grishin of Moscow, Georgy Romanov of Leningrad, and dozen of others from less significant provinces, were the most conservative part of the Soviet establishment, the epitome of its "totalitarian" character. "In Moscow they cut your nails, in Kiev they cut your fingers," was one Ukrainian dissident's comment on Shcherbitsky's policy at the time of perestroika.[14]

The ability to stage a protest has been pointed out by S. N. Eisenstadt as the prime feature of modernity, a proof of the existence of civil society under communist regimes.[15] However, the form in which communist societies protested was indicative of the opposite. The contagious quality of various discontents, if not immediately suppressed by force, derived from a lack of modern social divisions that might have counterbalanced the interests of particular groups. Therefore, the emergence, almost overnight, of the Solidarity movement of 10 million in Poland was hardly proof of a civil society simmering under the pressure of the communist regime. In fact, more systematic research found that the only two structures that attracted the individual loyalties of Poles in the seventies were "family" and "nation," with a peculiar vacuum in between, that is, in the space designated for the structures of civil society.[16]

Another stream of research on social modernization has stressed a different, and perhaps more important, role for civil society than staging a protest. These studies examined the process of political integration. The dominant theme of serious sociological research and theory, from Ferdinand Tönnies and Max Weber to Stein Rokkan and Seymour Martin Lipset, as well as some early works of S. N. Eisenstadt, concerned the changing cleavages and value commitments that pull individuals out of their primordial local-ethnic and kinship ties and integrate them into modern, nationwide, interconnected networks of interests and structures.[17] Rokkan, for example, demonstrated in many studies that the political integration of modern societies is based to a large extent on class and other modern cleavages, cutting across more traditional religious, ethnic, or regional ones.[18]

Rokkan's theory on the importance of cross-cutting cleavages in the process of political integration of modern societies received a peculiar confirmation after the collapse of communist regimes. The voting patterns in postcommunist elections hardly showed any consistent functional cleavages at the national level.[19] Accordingly, because of the lack of modern, functional divisions, postcommunist societies are prone to territorial fragmentation along primeval ethnic and regional lines. The same lack of vertical social structures has been pointed out as a major brake on the development of political parties.[20] The phenomenon of communist leaderships swept from power by overwhelming majorities in the first democratic elections only to return with narrow pluralities in the next ones, is another indication of the lack of a civil society that could challenge the remnants of the former ruling party.

The Communist State: Total or Incomplete?

Whatever might be said about totalitarian theory, its great impact on the popular image of communist regimes, including the self-image of their ruling strata, cannot be denied. As the model was losing credit in academia, it was gaining prominence in the popular imagination in the West and East alike. Perhaps the most impressive achievement of the totalitarian model was its resurrection as a symbol employed to mobilize communist societies against their already disintegrating regimes. Such use (or abuse) of a theory was bound to distort both the original concept and the reality it proposed to explain. Nevertheless, the totalitarian model became a political factor in itself. Thus, its authors can claim their parts in the East European revolutions, at least to the extent that Marx could be held responsible for the Bolshevik takeover.

The political import of totalitarian theory was all but fortuitous. The idea was politically loaded at its inception.[21] The fascist ideal of a total state was a romantic-conservative response to the appeal of revolutionary movements sweeping the Continent in the 1920s and 1930s. The idea of a total state was conceived as an alternative to the liberal doctrine of a minimal state, hence its openly anti-individualistic language.[22] At that time, liberal doctrine provided little practical guidance to young European nation-states approaching—and in some places plunging into—civil war. The flight of liberals to the right was as common in the Europe of the thirties as it has been in recent years in Russia.

The fascist doctrine of a total state never acquired serious academic credentials. Such acknowledgment occurred only thirty years later, when it was picked up—its ideological edge redirected —to denounce the nature of communist regimes. As a consistent theory, the totalitarian model has been a failure. Its first proponent, Hannah Arendt, did not attempt to construct such a theory in the first place.[23] She used the notion of totalitarianism to identify a certain historical phenomenon, namely, the messianic pan-movements that brought to life the regimes of Hitler and Stalin.

The subsequent version of the model by Carl Friedrich and Zbigniew Brzezinski was much more sterile.[24] Unfortunately, in their quest for scientific precision, these two authors sacrificed Arendt's brilliant insights and even twisted some of her major ideas. The main departure from Arendt in the Friedrich-Brzezinski model was the "etatisation" of the notion of totalitarianism. Arendt had never applied the term to states but to pan-movements and their parties. She repeatedly pointed to an antistatist bent as their major characteristic: "totalitarian parties hate states . . . they are parties above the state."[25] One of her most important insights was a distinction between two types of single-party regimes, depending on the position in which the party placed itself vis-à-vis the state.

In the first case the party considered itself above other parties but not above the state. This type was best represented by the Italian and some other fascist parties. Fascist movements were prostatist by nature, and they came to a halt the moment that the party seized power. In such cases the ruling elite may be replaced, but the administrative and economic structures do not need to be changed. The government remains the center of power, the party itself being "tied to the basically stable structure of the state," with a limited role similar to that of the "ministry of propaganda."

A different scenario applies, however, to a party that places itself not only above other parties but also above the state. According to Arendt, the Nazi and Bolshevik parties were cases in point. Both parties while in power attempted to maintain the momentum of their respective movements and imposed their own structures on the formal government. This effort resulted in a degradation of state institutions, since no stable administration could possibly meet the requirements of permanent combat and activist mobilization. Therefore, the administration, judiciary, and, above all, the state coercive forces became harnessed to the suprastate cause pursued by the party. The revolutionary character of totalitarian regimes also was stressed by Robert Tucker, who named them "movement-regimes."[26]

Thus, totalitarian parties conquer their respective states, appropriate the states' sovereignty, pulverize state administrations, leaving them empty shells. The classic study by Martin Broszat has shown how little of the coherent institutional framework usually associated with the notion of a "total state" was to be found in the Hitler state.[27] Juan J. Linz also pointed to the relationship between the state and the party as central to totalitarian rule. His conclusion was that "only when the party organization is superior or equal to the government can we speak of a totalitarian system."[28] Thus, for example, Linz did not consider the Franco regime in Spain totalitarian but authoritarian. Important differences between totalitarian and authoritarian regimes were further highlighted by Jeane Kirkpatrick.[29]

The uneasy relations between party and state hierarchies under totalitarian regimes were explained in Ernest Fraenkel's description of a "dual state" created on the Nazi takeover.[30] The party police agencies placed themselves in the position of what Fraenkel called the "normative state," whereas the regular administrative structure deteriorated to the subservient role of a "prerogative state." Although the judiciary and administration of the prerogative state had legally defined powers, it was left to the discretion of the normative state to impose its arbitrary decisions, the formal-legal procedures notwithstanding. As Fraenkel put it, the normative state was "competent in the matter of competence."[31]

The state's dubious position under the rule of a totalitarian party was even more distinct under communist regimes. Here, the very idea of a sovereign state was consigned to the famous dustbin of history, and the party was considered the only source of legitimate power. The ideal communist government drew its credentials from having been appointed, led, and supervised by the communist party. True, Stalin limited the party's arbitrary powers, but only to widen his own powers and not those of the state, which did little to secure the regime's institutional stability. Very much like Hitler, Stalin treated both state and party business as his personal affair, empowering his officials from case to case without any consistent division of labor, but solely on the basis of his own concerns.

Considering the peculiar fluidity of both Hitler's and Stalin's states, it is difficult to see how they could have been *total*. Nevertheless, in accord with the Friedrich-Brzezinski theory, the all-powerful, monolithic state became a trademark of the totalitarian model.[32] As it happened, such a version of totalitarianism came closer to the fascist origins of the term in bringing back the state as the main actor. It seems, however, that the totalitarian model also inherited a mystic disposition of its antecedent, a "total state," which was much boasted about by Mussolini but never really took shape.[33]

Further, the quest for scientific generalizations made Friedrich and Brzezinski lump together what Arendt had already managed to distinguish, that is, Italian Fascism, Franco's Spain, Hitler's Germany, and the subsequent governments of the Soviet Union. All those regimes were labeled with the same set of characteristics, whose number varied in subsequent refinements of the model. Some other totalitarian features were suggested, such as a drive toward world domination, the subjugation of legal order, and control of private morality, to mention just a few.[34] The next logical step in making the model more "scientific" was to add a quantitative dimension. Stanislav Andreski suggested a "totalitarian index" proportional to the scope of government control.[35] Since a government with nothing under its control cannot exist, it follows that all governments must be totalitarian to a degree. In this way a theory designed to distinguish a certain type of regime as unique ended up as a conceptual bridge among all kinds of regimes. In short, the more "scientific" the totalitarian theory became, the less it had to offer in explaining its own subject.

The deficiency of the totalitarian model resulted chiefly from a certain methodological problem of the social sciences, which was clarified by Max Weber. Weber criticized the peculiar hypostasy of some theoretical social science constructs, which purport to operate on historical developments with the same regularity and precision as the laws of nature.[36] Weber saw such a naturalistic approach to cultural phenomena as a gross distortion in social studies. For cultural phenomena are much less susceptible than natural ones to generic conceptualizations based on the classic formula *genus proximum, differentia specifica.* Since the social sciences are not based on axioms in the same way as the natural sciences, he wrote, the use of generic concepts by the social sciences must be greatly limited.

For the social sciences Weber devised a different method of conceptualization—his famous ideal type. I know of no social scientist who does not use the notion of the ideal type as an excuse whenever his or her model founders on hard data. In the above example of a "totalitarian index," Andreski also invokes the Weberian ideal type as he goes on to construct a classic generic concept, which was exactly what Weber repudiated in the social sciences. True, as Andreski has pointed out, Weber himself produced several generic concepts, but this does not change the validity of his criticism or the fact that his ideal type was clearly presented as an alternative to generic conceptualization.

Andreski has suggested giving up the difference between generic concepts and ideal types altogether and renaming generic concepts "pure types." An ideal type, he says, is a tautology anyway, since a type is ideal by definition. But that is exactly the point of Weber's method, which is about the "idealization of ideas." Ideal type is a method of identifying cultural objects (such as Christianity, capitalism, etc.) as historically unique phenomena and, because of their uniqueness, inaccessible to the generalization typical of natural sciences. Arendt's conception of totalitarianism identified a historical phenomenon and tried to distinguish its most typical features. In that, it was successful. Further versions of the model referred increasingly to a power as such, operating with the anonymity of natural forces, something that has never existed beyond the scholars' minds.

The failure of the totalitarian model was similar to the failure of modernization theory. Both concepts would have been capable of grasping the most distinct features of communist regimes if only they had remained faithful to the philosophical insights of their authors. Very much the same can be said about bureaucratic theory.

The Bureaucracy That Never Was

Bureaucratic interpretations of communist states may be divided into two categories. The first originated in radical Left critiques of Stalinism as a bureaucratic distortion of revolutionary ideas, and it has continued through the concepts of the "new ruling class" professed by the 1960s generation of revisionists.[37] The concept derived from the Marxist notion of bureaucracy as a parasitic, self-contained class, the servants of capital. In this sense the term bureaucracy was used as the antithesis to democracy, or more precisely to direct democracy.[38]

The second category of bureaucratic interpretations came from a technocratic vision of centrally planned societies. Here, the bureaucratic features of communist regimes resulted from the "rational management of social life by means of complex organization," and, in this sense, the conclusion was drawn that "communist systems look remarkably similar to bureaucratic organizations in other parts of the world."[39] This second interpretation opened Soviet studies to theories and methods already developed by a whole generation of students of institutional pathology such as Robert Merton, Talcott Parsons, Selznik, Crozier, and others.[40] The result was a popular understanding of communist regimes as enlarged cases of the bureaucratic oppression already well-known in the Western world. Both Marxist and liberal notions of bureaucracy are highly indiscriminate, derivative rather than analytical. Paul Hollander aptly described such use of the term as a "conceptual container," producing a "homogenizing approach towards all modern societies, communist and non-communist alike."[41]

It is difficult to understand why the notion of bureaucracy, one of the best-defined terms in the social sciences, should end up as such a conceptual container. Part of the misunderstanding can be traced to Weber's own writings. He used the term in various contexts, which sometimes were incompatible with his larger theory of classical bureaucracy. For example, Weber sometimes referred to various bureaucratic features appearing under patrimonial regimes,[42] which, by his own definition, could not sustain the formal-rational legal framework that makes bureaucracy possible in the first place.

Still more confusion came from Weber's famous warning about bureaucracy appropriating political power. This description has been applied to numerous regimes and seemed particularly well-suited to explain what was happening under communist governments. Using Weber's concept of bureaucracy in this way, however, means giving up his most important insights about modern administration. His warning about the bureaucratic acquisition of political power clearly concerned the system of *legal domination*. No other system places so much weight on legal expertise and procedural knowledge, which are the sources of bureaucratic power. The destruction of the body of laws leads, in turn, to a qualitatively different system, that of *personal domination*, under which neither legal rules nor a bureaucrat's knowledge matter enough to provide him with political power. Under such circumstances, a professional administrator becomes a secondary player; anyone's job may be taken over by a swiftly appointed commissar.

Weber saw the essence of bureaucratic organization not in its machinelike behavior (which was just a metaphor), but in its reliability compared to other forms of administration. Although modern bureaucratic efficiency largely stems from the professional training of its managers and the rational division of their competencies, it also derives from its ethos; without devotion to service and meticulous application of rules, for example, the machinery as a whole simply would not work. Apart from practical considerations, the formal-rational bureaucracy has proved to be an indispensable basis for both economic development and democracy. Reliance on general, impersonal rules known to everyone makes bureaucratic decisions predictable, and this predictability strengthens a stable framework within which economic enterprises may operate.[43]

A no less important side effect of modern bureaucracy is its leveling influence on society. The rejection of decision making in a case-by-case manner does away with traditional privileges and makes everyone legally equal. For these reasons, Weber thought that formal-rational bureaucracy was both an indispensable and permanent feature of modern societies. In contrast to some socialist and anarchist arguments, Weber believed that modern societies cannot dispense with bureaucracy or replace it with something better. The tasks usually performed by modern states cannot be carried out other than by expert training, functional specialization, and efficient coordination, that is, by formally rational bureaucratic administration.

True, during the Stalin era the notion of revolutionary legal nihilism was refuted, and a more stable pattern of authority was established.[44] The fastidious documentation left behind by Stalin's apparatus of terror testifies to his efforts to acquire a proper bureaucracy. However, massive paperwork is not all that bureaucracy is about. What was missing in Stalin's regime was a stable legal system valid for all levels of government, including its highest reaches. Therefore, neither Stalin's concept of "socialist law" nor his constitution could possibly make the communist administration into a bureaucratic type.

In the post-Stalin era the communist apparatus of power acquired some internal rules that limited the personal arbitrariness of Soviet leaders.[45] Nevertheless, the principle of democratic centralism, which provided for the suspension of any rules in favor of the leadership's current orders was never abolished, not even by Gorbachev when he sought to introduce a "legal state" in the USSR. In fact, Gorbachev's reforms of Soviet government never went much further than those of Stalin; in both cases the role of the party diminished, but only to increase the leader's arbitrary power.

Had it been applied in its Weberian meaning, the concept of bureaucracy might have been a powerful instrument to single out the most important feature that distinguished a communist government from other modern governments—that is, the role of the legal system. However, since the notion of bureaucracy more often has been applied in its Marxist derivative meaning (as a parasitic class), this difference was lost. The resulting confusion had important consequences for the practice of communist regimes. Having been disappointed by the performance of their administrations, communist leaders repeatedly launched antibureaucratic campaigns to improve them. But a classical bureaucracy—that is, a reliable and impersonal machinery of administration—was exactly what they were trying to achieve, and this could not be established by the revolutionary means of antibureaucratic campaigns.

Whatever incipient rules had taken root in the Soviet apparatus of power during periods of stagnation, they were lifted in the course of subsequent antibureaucratic campaigns, thus sending the regime back into its liquid, prebureaucratic stage. This was particularly relevant to Gorbachev's perestroika, which in one sweep did away with the causes of stagnation and the country's only entrenched administrative structures.

The Party-State Relationship: The Rules of Demarcation and Domination

Raymond Aron characterized communist societies as "ideocratic." That feature merged political and semireligious institutions, and it derived from Byzantine traditions. Ernest Gellner, in turn, found some parallels in the Caesaro-papist moments of Western Christianity when the head of the church tried to rule the Holy Empire: "Church and state possess parallel and intertwining hierarchies, with personnel moving between the two, and the church dominant overall."[46]

In fact, Lenin's prescription for the party-state relationship closely resembled the rules of demarcation and domination established in the eleventh century by Gregorian reformers to guide relations between the spiritual power of the church and the secular power of the king. Such a "constitutional theory" has two dominant characteristics. First, according to the rule of demarcation, the party is not supposed to replace the state, lest the party finds itself reduced to a merely coercive force, which, according to its own ideology, is the ultimate nature of all states, including those of workers and peasants. Second, according to the rule of domination, the source of legitimate authority resides solely in the party. This meant that the state's traditional legitimacy has to be challenged, even if that legitimacy is employed time and again by the party itself.

Although applying the rules of demarcation and domination was by no means homogeneous at all times and places, the practice was nowhere as important as the professed principle that a "secular" authority of the state is not legitimate by itself. For several reasons, the analogy between the church and the communist party cannot be pursued much further. Perhaps the most important reason was the different impacts of the two institutions on their respective societies. The heritage of legal culture enabled the Roman Catholic Church to play a constructive role in the European state-building processes. No communist party can be credited with similar achievements.

In practice, party-state relations in communist countries varied, depending on place, time, and level of hierarchy. As a rule, the party's ascendancy over territorial administration was stronger than over the central government, for the institutional distinctions were clearer in the center than in the provinces. In some regions and times the power of party bosses within their fiefdoms was more comprehensive than the power of the top national leaders, since the local bosses had less complex circumstances and interests to reckon with. In the post-Stalinist era, in particular, an integrated local elite was able to dominate all local positions of importance, thus rendering the elaborate institutional framework meaningless.

The best way to research this subject is to test the turnover in the regional headquarters of the most important all-union institutions against the turnover in the regional party executive bodies (the little politburos). Since the mid-sixties the composition of the regional and republican politburos had been relatively stable, even though individual members kept changing their institutional

affiliation.[47] For example, one person might have kept his membership in the regional party executive, at first as chairman of the presidium of the local soviet, and eventually as chairman of the party control commission. Another would do the same, first in his capacity as director of a large industrial plant, and subsequently as head of the industry department in the regional party committee.

The phenomenon of the "jobs roundabout" within the regions bore some resemblance to the former Stalinist tactics applied at the center. Stalin moved his regional secretaries from one place to another to prohibit their *territorial entrenchment*, whereas a regional party leader of the post-Stalinist era shifted his subordinates from one institution to another to prevent their *institutional entrenchment*. This tactic was perhaps the principal mechanism of centralization within the regions, which made institutional divisions at the regional level more apparent than real, while causing the local elite to be fairly resistant to departmental manipulations from the center.

Further, it is said that the central government grew in strength under Stalin. True, Stalin's "revolution from above" and the mass terror that followed coincided roughly with the partial restoration of traditional patterns of authority.[48] Revolutionary justice was denounced, and its protagonists joined their former victims in gulags. This looked like a classic state-building enterprise. The war effort and the subsequent Soviet victory in 1945 seemed at first to further the restoration of a "normal" Russian autocratic state. But Stalin was a mediocre state-builder; he multiplied institutions with overlapping jurisdictions, installed special commissars with competing powers, and later he denounced his entire administration to the public as a bunch of corrupt "bureaucrats." The turf battles resulting from such practices widened his personal power but did little in the way of building the state.

The state came under ideological attack again when Nikita Khrushchev fought his rivals, who all happened to hold major state posts. In his secret speech to the Twentieth Congress of the CPSU in 1956, Khrushchev made the state the chief perpetrator of the Stalinist errors and distortions, which he explained away as an excessive use of the "administrative means" resulting from the overgrowth of state powers.[49] The party came out of this diagnosis as the prime victim of the state, and Khrushchev was determined to restore the party's power and glory according to Leninist principles (described above). This leitmotif was consistently developed in the program that he presented in 1961, according to which the state was to wither away as its functions were progressively taken over by social organizations. Such an evaluation was widely accepted both by party apparatchiks throughout the Eastern bloc and by inner-party Marxist "revisionist" critics, who saw Stalinism as a special form of bureaucracy.

Khrushchev used this "party ideology" as the means of factional infighting. His target was the antiparty group, consisting of leftovers from Stalin's government (Nikolay Bulganin, Georgy Malenkov, Lazar Kaganovich, and Kliment Voroshilov). Each of them happened to hold a leading government position and stood in Khrushchev's way in reviving the party's traditionally dominant role. As soon as the antiparty group was defeated in 1958, Khrushchev assumed the post of prime minister, while still holding, like Stalin, the position of general secretary.

The option between the state and party dictatorship was not purely abstract. In the case of state dictatorship, the party is left with meager powers of the "ministry of propaganda," whereas in the party dictatorship it possesses all the means of administration, which in the post-Stalinist regime, when the role of terror diminished, provided an important instrument of power. Thus, Khrushchev's affirmation of Leninist principles — that is, the supremacy of the party apparatus over government machinery — had important consequences for the future of communist regimes.

The long-term result of Khrushchev's reforms was the weakening of vertical channels of command outside the party that previously had been boosted by Stalin. First of all, ministries were stripped of their intermediate structures, and their provincial offices were either abolished or subordinated to the soviets, people's councils, communes, and similar agencies of "council democracy." This act was tantamount to the parallel party committees' extensive control of territorial administration. The police forces preserved their separate hierarchies, but they were open to lateral supervision from party committees at all levels. Thus, communist parties became polymorphic, with their organs penetrating all of the remaining institutions at all levels of the administrative hierarchy.[50]

Students of those developments have sometimes queried how it happened that the party finally reasserted its dominance over the government machinery, which it had lost to some extent under Stalin. Some allowance must be made for the personal energy and skills of Khrushchev. Further, as Leonard Schapiro pointed out, "in a system where policy is largely formulated independently of public opinion and where genuine representative organs for resolving the differences of view between several leaders of equal status do not exist, a dictatorship of one man offers the advantages of efficiency and convenience." However, that does not answer the question of why party and not state dictatorship would bring this "advantage of efficiency and convenience." An answer may be found in the issue of legitimacy.

A formal government possesses its own traditional legitimacy, independent of and even in opposition to the legitimacy of the party. Whenever this traditional state legitimacy came to the fore, the fortunes of the whole communist establishment were gravely exposed. Such was the lesson of the Hungarian uprising in 1956, when an unimpressive apparatchik, Imre Nagy, was able to mobilize wide popular support after he was appointed prime minister; from that position he was able to challenge the entire party leadership. The leaders of ruling communist parties have always been aware of this lesson and have taken appropriate care to prevent the formal government from accruing excessive powers. In particular, the army and police forces were placed under the close supervision of mixed party-state bodies.

In the economy the interlocking party-state hierarchies are said to have been instrumental in mobilizing the resources necessary to fulfill production targets. In this context, Richard Bendix explained the rationale of this double hierarchy, with a party functionary placed at the side of every major official to prevent concealment and apply pressure:

Indeed, the two hierarchies would be required even if all key positions in government and industry were filled with party functionaries. For a functionary turned executive official would still be responsible for "overfulfilling" the plan, while the new party functionary who took his place would still be charged with keeping the official under pressure and surveillance.[51]

Merle Fainsod called this organizational device "institutionalization of mutual suspicion."[52] In a wider context it was a typical feature of arbitrary rule, where clever tactics of control are mixed with organizational mess and ineptness.[53] For there were more hierarchies than just those of the party and state. Within the party itself, separate hierarchies of the party control commissions were linked to the political police, which, needless to say, had a hierarchy of its own. Further, mixed party-state bodies such as worker and peasant inspectorates and a plethora of other task groups and committees plus swiftly appointed commissars were sent from the center to check on the entire apparatus.

Nevertheless, conflicts between party and state leaders happened time and again. After the war, Stalin assumed leadership in both party and state hierarchies, and communist leaders in other Soviet bloc countries followed suit. Soon after Stalin's death, however, Khrushchev presented these leaders with a tough choice between either state or party positions. All of them made the right choice for party leadership. One exception was the Bulgarian leader, Georgyu Dej, who kept the premiership and appointed the most harmless of his collaborators, Todor Zhivkov, as first secretary. Zhivkov's dimwitted demeanor became a standing joke at gatherings of the fraternal parties. It did not prevent him, however, from becoming the longest-ruling (1953–1990) of all communist leaders.

The last example of a general secretary winning supremacy over the prime minister was the Brezhnev-Kosygin duel at the end of the 1960s. After Aleksey Kosygin's reforms fizzled out (see chapter 2), the CPSU's dominant role went unchallenged for the next twenty years—until Gorbachev's perestroika.

The Administration of Terror

To be sure, terror was a powerful instrument to fill institutional gaps, but administering terror posed its own problems. In particular, communist leaders used to face a dilemma concerning the relationship between the hierarchies of the security services and the party apparatus. The dilemma consisted of a narrow choice between a self-contained hierarchy of the security forces subordinated directly to the general secretary, and horizontal subordination of security services at each territorial level to the corresponding party committee. A mixture of the two was possible, but a stable and uniform framework for this vital relationship had never been established.

The first solution seemed to be the most effective, since it provided an extra check on the party apparatus and stiffened its discipline. However, a paradox of arbitrary rule appears in that the more reliance placed by a leader on the forces of coercion, the more dependent he becomes on them.[54] In the long run, only a gifted ruler can manage such a dependence. When it happens, the security services acquire ascendancy over all other departments of government and threaten the ruling elite itself. A situation of this kind was inherited by Stalin's successors, who sought a solution in partially subordinating the security services to the regional party leaders.

The territorial principle under arbitrary rule involves risks of its own, however. Party and police officials may consolidate at the local level, and soon the process of territorial fragmentation sets in. Yuri Andropov fought hard to defend the integrity of the KGB's ranks when he chaired that institution in the seventies. Nevertheless, the two largest republics (after the Russian Federation), the Ukraine and Kazakhstan, developed into semi-emancipated fiefdoms with the local KGB in close collusion with the party apparatus. During the second year of Gorbachev's rule, the removal of the Kazakh leader caused major disturbances. The Ukrainian party leader, Vladimir Shcherbitsky, maintained his position almost until the end, together with his membership in the Politburo—his open hostility toward perestroika notwithstanding.

The "Etatisation" of the Party

As communist ideology was wearing out, state legitimacy was re-emerging. In the mid-1970s communist parties legitimized their leading role by enshrining it in their state constitutions. This constitutional blessing might have seemed a mere embellishment for a despotic regime. Nevertheless, when the emergence of Solidarity in Poland challenged the party's ideological claims to represent the workers, party leaders could step forward in their role as defenders of the "state and constitution." The leading party sociologists (Jerzy Wiatr, for example) maintained that the ruling party was in fact performing the function of state authority. Consequently, a certain degree of influence from rank-and-file party members on the leadership (even if purely theoretical) should be regarded as a kind of social control exercised over the government.[55]

All of these theoretical and constitutional exercises did not change the original principle about the state's subservient role to the party. Even in Poland, where the etatisation of the communist regime was fairly advanced toward the end of the regime, the party apparatus was taught that the reasons for the state's preservation were purely instrumental; the state was needed to authorize acts of coercion and to perform more specialized functions in the economy, as such economic necessities "proved more complex than Lenin had initially thought."[56] However, the textbook stated unequivocally that "the division of work by no means implies the division of power."[57]

Communist Government in Weberian Conceptualization: A "Missing Type"

Several attempts have been made to classify communist governments as a mixture of rational, traditional, and charismatic types.
Along these lines, Kenneth Jowitt developed a concept of the
Leninist party as a "collective hero," an amalgam of traditional
and modern elements simultaneously representing "bureaucratic
discipline and charismatic correctness."[58] The party extends its
powers by including different social groups and activities, all of
which are absorbed into its political interests, thus preventing the
development of public and economic realms in their own right.
In this sense, the regime refused the modern differentiation of
political, economic, and social spheres and drifted toward a kind
of patriarchal neotraditionalism.

It should be noted, however, that the Weberian types of authority (rational, traditional, and charismatic) are based on both
the mode of organization and the type of legitimacy—legitimacy
meaning the popular beliefs that sustain a given system. Those
beliefs provide "the basis upon which the officials obey the ruling
minority and the people at large obey both."[59] The presence of
these beliefs thus makes a real difference. In this context, the role
of ideology becomes paramount. It not only provides the necessary cement for the ruling elite (or self-legitimacy), but it also
sets limits to organizational choice.

Perhaps ideology's most important role was its suspension of all
legal and traditional norms, thereby abolishing the rudimentary
criteria of legitimacy. Bendix concluded that a communist regime
remains "clearly outside Weber's tripartite division."[60] Nevertheless, he saw a possibility of applying some Weberian concepts
in the interpretation of communist government. In particular,
Weber's concept of substantive rationality, which was regarded
as the "missing type" in his conceptualization of political orders,
might apply.[61] The concept itself was left unfinished. Only scat-
tered remarks can be found in Weber's discussions of modern

communist movements and centrally planned economies as well as other systems "concerned with more or less 'just' economic distribution."[62]

In contrast to formally rational institutions oriented toward generalized and impersonal rules, such as the market or bureaucracy, the substantively rational institutions are based on some overwhelming moral, political, or religious commitment. To be sure, no actual regime, including that of legal domination, can dispense with some elements of substantive rationality. For the goals of policy, which are value-oriented by definition, cannot be derived from purely formal considerations. In the "missing-type" hypothesis, however, a purely substantive norm—for example, an ideology—makes both the formal-legal and the traditional rules redundant. This redundancy, in turn, leads to augmenting the personal discretion of those who rule in the name of ideological objectives. Therefore, when attempting to explain a communist government, it seems more fruitful to search for the exigencies of arbitrary power than for any type of legitimacy.

Chapter 6

Despotism and

the Modern State

When the savages of Louisiana are desirous of fruit, they cut the tree at the root, and gather the fruit. This is an emblem of despotic government. —Montesquieu, *The Spirit of the Laws*

The communist experiment demonstrated what happens when the state is in fact reduced to sheer force and modern social divisions are eradicated by means of mass dispossession. The regime tends to disintegrate. For the exigencies of arbitrary power are much more complex than totalitarian theory has ever attempted to examine. Max Weber described the paradox of a despotic ruler who rejects all traditional and legal constraints on his powers only to discover that the reticence of his own officials limits his freedom of action even more severely; arbitrary powers of the center are replicated at all levels of administration, thereby undermining the center's discretion.[1] Montesquieu summarized this phenomenon in the memorable phrase: "In fine, as the law is the momentary will of the prince, it is necessary that those who will for him should follow his sudden manner of willing."[2]

In short, the Soviet Union fragmented and collapsed not because it contained many nationalities and was economically declining, although these things helped, but because it was despotic. What renders despotism unworkable in modern societies is the logic of the administrative process, that is, the need to delegate a great many tasks and make sure that those tasks are done well. The story of perestroika shows how little Gorbachev had in the way of a coherent institutional setting when he tried to find a base for reform. The Soviet state, far from being "total," was incomplete, its structures having neither autonomy nor distinctiveness. As for the party, although its apparatus simulated certain traits of a stringent bureaucracy, it could hardly perform its typical integrative role, lacking as it did the bureaucratic ethos and reliability. Thus, the state's weakness, rather than its omnipotence, stalled communist projects of modernization and, most notably, Gorbachev's perestroika. Gorbachev's failure only sealed a more general failure of communist regimes—*their inability to build a modern state.*

State and Revolution

If the state was only an organizer of political domination for the privileged, as Marxists like to believe, it should make little difference what kind of organization does the job for the dominant class, be it a single party, the "paid servants of capital," or a mafia. However, the state also plays an important role as a guarantor of the general interests of those that it governs. If this universal role is to be fulfilled, the state ought to be relatively autonomous from other institutions.[3] In many ways, the efficiency of a modern state is contingent on its autonomy and distinctiveness from other institutions. Autonomy also is essential for popular legitimacy as well as for the morale of the "administrative class." Indeed, the more a given set of policies operates independently of market forces, the greater the need for autonomous institutions to carry out these policies and to stand up to dominant interest groups that seek to use them for their own ends.

Perfect autonomy of the state is impossible given the presence of various pressure groups inside and outside government. Further, pockets of neopatrimonialism have persisted even in the most developed countries and institutions. The impact of tradition, charismatic personalities, and informal power relations cannot be eradicated completely, even under well-entrenched formal-legal systems. Only the pressure of competition keeps both political and economic institutions on their toes and forces them to cultivate and develop their modern features, such as financial discipline, meritocratic criteria of selection and promotion, etc. Communist governments made sure that no such pressures affected them.

Communist governments apparently had all the means of effective state-building at their disposal. First, nationalization of the entire economy put them in control of most of their countries' resources. Also, their freedom to choose particular venues of production and redistribution was relatively unrestricted by either political or economic factors; neither free elections nor market forces swayed the decisions of party leadership. Further, the absence of competition from other political parties ensured that the center was able to consolidate quickly, which is another precondition for top-down state-building. Finally, the party apparatus was selected in a way that made it relatively homogeneous and, at least theoretically, dependent on the center for individual careers.

Yet the actual success of communist parties in securing for themselves a centralized and reliable machinery of administration was not impressive. Centralized institutions are not part of a natural order, nor can they be established by decree or purely by coercive measures. Effective centralization is a relatively new phenomenon and has been achieved by means of modern integrative factors, such as a working legal system, a professional administration selected on merit, and a manageable economy based on money and markets with their multifarious effects on social structures and mobility.

Communist governments had none of these legal and economic instruments of a modern state at their disposal, having deliberately discarded them into the dustbin of history right at the beginning of their rule. Instead, they strove to concentrate their powers by the crude means of terror, aggressive deployment of personnel, and frequent incursions into organizational charters. Indeed, the very meaning of "administration" became tantamount to coercion. For example, the mass killings of the Stalin era were diagnosed by Nikita Khrushchev as an excessive reliance on "administrative means." Such use of this term was adopted by all communist parties and was interpreted by outsiders as yet another piece of party jargon. In fact, it reflected the communist understanding of what administration is about.

Administration implies relatively stable structures and procedures vested with a measure of legitimacy, whereas communist leaders usually considered it in terms of a short-term organizational task rather than a long-term institutional one. Constant changes in administrative structures, functions, and units set the territorial systems of communist countries into flux, which greatly contributed to their repeated failures.

The legal and financial institutions of the modern state actually did wither away under the early years of communist rule. Communist modernization was performed by means typical of a patrimonial estate rather than a modern economy and administration. In all countries that came under communist rule all the legal and financial institutions were dismantled right in the beginning of the new regime.[4] As projects of industrialization advanced under Stalin, armies of professional administrators, managers, and other specialists were marched to the gulags and their places taken by semiliterate party hacks. The result was a recurrent failure of economic and administrative performance whenever objectives could not be achieved by force. This failure, in turn, made communist leaders prone to resuscitate revolutionary methods as means of reform.

Such revolutions from above were usually launched as antibureaucratic campaigns, which occurred repeatedly in all communist countries. Their purpose was to instigate popular outrage against local apparatchiks, who had chosen to pursue their own goals instead of carrying out orders from the center.

But just as the diagnosis of the malady was wrong, so was the cure. Bureaucracy in its genuine Weberian sense is an impersonal, rule-implementing, and specialized administrative machine, a key agent in the state-building process. That machinery was precisely what communist governments lacked. Throughout its history the Soviet administrative machinery remained shaky, unstructured, and prone to territorial fragmentation. Any incipient rules that had taken root in the apparatus of power during periods of stagnation were lifted during subsequent antibureaucratic campaigns, sending the regime back into its liquid, prebureaucratic form. Thus, a gap developed between the increasing complexity of an industrial economy and society on the one hand and the crude means of administration on the other.

It was no accident that a relatively complex industrial economy was supervised by means of a primitive, preindustrial administration. Such administration was encumbered by the regime's pivotal designs, that is, the Marxist idea of the state and the Leninist principle of rule by the party.

Administrative Utopia and One-Party Dictatorship

The unraveling regime provides an opportunity to see more clearly its latent and most persistent features, which make it incapable of coping with mounting challenges. Such features often may be tracked down to the visions and obsessions of the founding fathers and to the rudiments of organizations from which the regime was spawned.

The evolution of communist regimes reflects a constant search for a viable government to accommodate arbitrary powers. It was furnished by two devices. The first was the semianarchic framework of "council democracy," which made formal-legal restraints on authority meaningless. The second was the principle of central planning, which gave political authorities direct access to national resources without legal or financial constraints. Both principles were intertwined in the initial projects of the founding fathers, Marx and Lenin. The self-administered "commune state" was to serve a libertarian cause. The technocratic vision of a centrally planned "labor state" was to secure the abundance and just distribution of goods.[5] It is said that the libertarian model reflected the original intentions of the founding fathers, whereas the centrally planned, dictatorial regime came as a political necessity.

In fact, the historical evolution of both Marx's and Lenin's programs went the other way round. While studying in the quiet repose of libraries, both men came to appreciate the "bourgeois state" for its capacity to concentrate power and wealth. The founding fathers were not anarchist, far from it. In their initial plans state machinery with all the banks and cartels was not to be destroyed but usefully employed for the right cause. The reconciliation of Marx and Lenin with anarchism came later when it appeared that the business of government was too difficult for revolutionaries to handle. This problem occurred to Marx in 1848, when he observed the Paris Commune. His conclusion was that "the working class cannot simply lay hold of the ready-made State machinery, and wield it for its own purposes." Therefore, instead of a "proletarian coup d'état," the revolution was to result in "the abolition of the state hierarchy" and "the resumption of its authority by the masses themselves."[6]

A similar change of mind could be detected in Lenin's program. During his Finnish exile Lenin had a radical change of mind about the shape of revolutionary government, which surprised his comrades at the time and has remained a mystery. From a dogmatic, highly centralistized vision of the dictatorship of the proletariat, he moved to a semi-anarchic model of a commune state. This change may be more easily understood if one considers the Bolsheviks' unwillingness to take up a government for which they felt insufficiently prepared.[7] One of Lenin's comrades went so far as to lock himself in his apartment, refusing to come out until he was certain that no one would force him to become a minister. Lenin probably wrote his pamphlet *State and Revolution* to dispel his comrades' doubts about their abilities to govern. His idea that anybody could govern (even a housewife, providing that he or she had a proper, proletarian consciousness) was truly revolutionary at the time, and it required a proper ideological justification. The way that Lenin made his case transcended his original purpose; his pamphlet, *State and Revolution,* became an inspiration for generations of revolutionaries to come.

Apparent contradictions between the semi-anarchic model of self-administered communes and the requirements of a centrally planned society have been pointed out as the prime causes of the failure of communist regimes to deliver on their promises. The problem was not, however, that the initial projects were contradictory and therefore did not work; rather, they worked only too well, their theoretical incompatibility notwithstanding. For both designs had common features that in practice made them compatible.

First, both communal and centrally planned societies are essentially nondemocratic, at least in a formal sense of democracy. In the process of central planning, social interests are to be calculated in a scientific manner, whereas in the commune state, the knowledge of what is good for society is to be secured by a nonempirical process (general will, "correct consciousness," etc.). Negotiating and voting on social policies makes little sense if those policies are to be established by scientific means.[8] Also, the general will does not need to coincide with the will of the majority, and correct consciousness may be possessed by only a few.

Second, both kinds of societies can dispense with separate legislative, executive, and juridical institutions. In the centrally planned society those functions were to be absorbed by the economic administration. The commune, in turn, signified the fusion of legislative, judicial, and executive powers with the population at large. Indeed, separate state institutions are not needed in a society that can articulate its interests in a direct and unequivocal manner, especially if those interests are presumed to be uniform.

Finally, the prime target of both projects was the state with its command over people's loyalties. The technocratic model was supranational; central planning was to expand to a European-wide or even worldwide scale. The communal model, in turn, was designed to break up the centralized nation-state from below into a multitude of self-governing units, each a political center of its own. Thus, both projects embraced a new constitutional framework for a society that would dispense with the political authority of the state altogether.

From Discussion to Dictatorship

The Soviet experiment was welcomed as a "new epoch state" by some participants in the contemporary Weimar constitutional debate, and they proposed a similar type of "associational" organization based on self-government.[9] This new epoch state came under scathing criticism from Carl Schmitt. He did not believe that the question of sovereignty would disappear under an associational or any other constitution but would become only more intractable when removed from official doctrine. Schmitt predicted that "the solution of such historical-pedagogical problems often takes an unexpected turn from discussion to dictatorship."[10]

The first large-scale implementation of a new epoch state in the Soviet Union confirmed Schmitt's prediction. The semi-anarchic pattern of the soviets proved readily compatible with the dictatorial drive of the Leninist party. Thanks to their vague constitutions and flexible, nonbureaucratic procedures, the soviets provided the Bolsheviks with a suitable legitimacy for one-party dictatorship. The merger of legislative, executive, and judicial powers typical of "council democracy" was especially helpful, since it removed formal-legal restrictions on authority. The principle of central planning, in turn, gave the party direct access to physical and human resources without legal and financial responsibilities attached to a contract. Thus, it was not that the design of the founding fathers failed to work—the problem was that it did work.

The result was a despotic government with distinct, premodern features such as insufficient control over the forces of coercion in the center and the growing strength of local barons in the provinces. Since the regime lacked its own engine of internal development, it was propelled by repeated revolutions from above that were employed by more resourceful leaders. But what a patrimonial regime needs is the cultivation of its traditions and routines rather than a revolutionary change that destroys them. In this sense, the revolutionary tenet so successfully employed as a means of concentration of power proved fatal in the long run for the internal stability of the Soviet regime. As a revolutionary, Mikhail Gorbachev soon ran short of options. But when he turned conservative, he found he had precious little left to conserve.

Gorbachev's Conservative Revolution

Perestroika aimed at the reconstruction of central powers, both political and economic, and in this sense Gorbachev's objectives did not deviate from the basic principles of the Soviet regime. He did not intend to change the regime's patrimonial features, as he knew no others, but only to take a better hold of its machinery. However, once countervailing centers develop in the peripheries, their peaceful neutralization is difficult if not impossible.

The story of perestroika consists of defensive actions taken by various parts of the apparatus of power in response to the precipitate policies of the new leadership. The republican and regional leaders, treated by Gorbachev to glasnost and popular elections, turned to nationalism and localism as the tactics of personal survival. Regardless of whether they had managed to win local support (as in Central Asia) or found themselves overwhelmed by already thriving national fronts (as in the Baltics), the regime's horizontal sinews between the center and the republics became severely exposed. The surgery was completed by Boris Yeltsin when he set up the Russian government and obtained democratic legitimacy for it.

The presence of the alternative Russian government at the time of the August 1991 coup contributed greatly to the tumbling of the Soviet edifice. Had it not been for the folly of "putchisty," this edifice would have had a chance of enduring for some time, thus making the post-Soviet transition different from what it is now.

In the long run, hostilities between the two pillars of the Soviet regime, the KGB and the military, were still more momentous, wearing down the center, parallel to and independent of territorial disintegration. Old feuds die hard, and they may prevent alliances that are in the best interests of the parties involved. Instead of closing ranks in time of crisis, the KGB and the military took advantage of the regime's loosened control to settle their accounts, not realizing how obsolete their feuds were. The war of attrition between the two principal Soviet establishments assured their mutual destruction.

The fact that the army was destroyed first and the KGB only afterward (and only for lack of military support) substantially affected later developments. If Yugoslavia was an example of an army let loose after the collapse of a communist regime, the Soviet Union exemplified a disintegrating police state. The type of anarchy that follows from these two scenarios is different. Instead of open civil war as in Yugoslavia, in Russia the civil war is covert.

A Look into the Abyss

The change of generations in power made the greatest impact on the communist apparatus. Western Sovietologists expected the new generation to perform the final act of convergence with liberal democracy, preserving at the same time the "socialist values" of the initial project. How could they do all this, though, knowing so little about the regime that they were supposed to reform?

The rewriting of history proved most damaging to the ability of Soviet leaders to predict the consequences of democratization and new international relations after the cold war. Confronted with a series of national rebellions, the Russians could not understand the strong resentments of peoples that they believed to be beneficiaries rather than victims of the empire. Such illusions may have been the norm for all imperial societies and the major source of postimperial identity crises, such as those that Britain and France had gone through. What makes the Russian postimperial crisis much more acute is that the basic values and identity of many millions of people were inextricably tied to the ideology of their multinational empire.

As children we were glad that practically nothing was left of old pre-Revolutionary Russia. . . . We sincerely believed that other peoples would never be happy until they did what we did, until they followed us, until they demolished their cathedrals, did away with merchants, private enterprises, rich farmers, until they became exactly as we were. . . . We thought we had tied our lives to a great truth . . . we were pioneers leading the rest of mankind to the realm of freedom and spiritual blessing, but we have come to realise that our way is the way to nowhere . . . that we were purposefully engaging in self-destruction.[11]

Not many can afford such an admission and live on with the knowledge that one's life was based on a deception. That is why the cataclysmic history of the Soviet Union remains in Russia in a state of semioblivion.

Stories of gulags, famines, mass deportations, and killing fields, after initially exciting public curiosity, no longer sell well. The facts are well known, anyway; almost every Soviet citizen over fifty has his or her story to tell. What is lacking is a shared conception of the meaning of these facts, as if a culture with its norms and ethos was erased from social memory altogether. That is why comparisons with Weimar or post-Nazi Germany are superficial. The German retreat into barbarism was brief and left behind plenty of cultural ground on which to reconstruct the social fabric. In Russia, by contrast, three generations already have grown up with little or no memory of what it was like before the great rupture. No such case of collective amnesia over more than seventy years can be found in the whole of history as we know it.

As for Soviet culture, it might have been "ironic" (to borrow Ernest Gellner's notion) for the last twenty or so years of the regime, meaning that official ideology was taken by the public with a pinch of salt; however, that culture did provide some guidelines for everyday life and a measure of mutual understanding within society. The consequences of the sudden invalidation of such established conceptions of life and society—as happened after the dissolution of the Soviet Union—are difficult to comprehend.

Epilogue

Europe is coming out of its latest war of religions. The previous one in the seventeenth century gave the West its doctrine of political authority. The Catholic-Protestant conflict demonstrated a need for the highest arbiter at home and legitimized the sovereign authority of the state. At the same time, the Peace of Westphalia introduced an important division between the public and private spheres; it gave rulers the right to oversee public policy on religion, but their subjects preserved the right to follow their own beliefs in private. Although this formula of a sovereign but tolerant state was often abused, it became the foundation for the West European nation-states; it legitimized both the sovereign authority of the state and the individual rights of people living under the state's jurisdiction.

The peoples of East Central Europe did not participate in this 1648 settlement but remained subject to imperial centers for the next two centuries. Only in another Thirty Years War, the one of 1914 to 1944, did they become exposed to political modernity. In this sense, Yalta was for Eastern Europe what the Peace of Westphalia was for the West. But it was a different political philosophy altogether, one that dispensed with both sovereign states and individual rights.

The intellectual response to the Western experience of civil wars was summarized in *Leviathan*. The Hobbesian alternative between a despotic government and the war of everyone against everyone else, though seemingly logical, proved false; instead of *Leviathan*, the West acquired democracy and pluralism. In Eastern Europe the state has been condemned as the major culprit, first by Marxist dogma, and then by totalitarian theory processed into a simple opposition between state and society. Civil society, in a somewhat eschatological version, has been proclaimed by the philosophers of East European revolutions to be the best guardian of liberalism and democracy. Is there a Leviathan waiting to prove intellectuals wrong again?

Making the state responsible for the abuses of a totalitarian regime not only misrepresented its nature but also had an impact on postcommunist reforms. For democratic reforms and a market economy to flourish, a working machinery of government is necessary. As Carl Friedrich put it, before limited government can be installed, there first has to be a government with powers to limit.[1] Communist parties did away with states without building a single institution that was not an extension of the party itself. In such circumstances, deliberations on the constitutional division of powers seem abstract, since after disabling the party few institutions have been left to exercise those powers. In this respect, Russia is at a clear disadvantage toward its former satellites, which at least had a brief period of modern state-building between the world wars.

The first assignment of the first democratic governments in postcommunist societies has been to build state structures, but as soon as they begin this task, accusations of "totalitarianism" are being hurled at them.

The Germans have had the Machiavellian Fortuna clearly on their side. The Caucasian miracle can only be compared to another that happened in January 1762 when the disastrous Silesian adventure of Frederick the Great threatened the very survival of Prussia as an independent state. At the critical moment, when the Russian and Austrian forces were about to strike the last blow, Russian Tsarina Elizabeth died. Her successor, Peter III, was a great admirer of things Prussian. He gave up all Russian acquisitions in Prussia and recommended to his ally a speedy conclusion of peace. This sudden reversal of Russian-Prussian relations marked the beginning of the rapid development of Prussia, and later Germany, as a European power. From then on, Prussian and Russian imperial interests in Central Europe became a bridge of understanding between the two powers, a union of interests that was sealed by the partition of Poland.

The Russian empire survived longer into the twentieth century than any other, given an additional lease on life by victory in World War II. But imperial endurance also meant a delay in building a modern state. The weaknesses of the empire's internal structures have always made the rulers of Russia fear that "unless the empire expanded, it would implode."[2] When the Atlantic system of collective security imposed external limits on Soviet expansion, the regime at first stagnated and then collapsed in on itself before the eyes of those who tried to reform it.

The slow progress in sciences and technology, and the fact that this deficiency threatened the Soviet position in the arms race, reportedly influenced Gorbachev's elite to reform the petrified regime. But developments in the social sciences also had some impact on the agenda of perestroika. Being "scientific" by nature, communist regimes were susceptible to vagaries in the social sciences. This vulnerability was spotted by Ernest Gellner when he commented on the difficulties of disconnecting from current developments in science a doctrine that had scientific pretensions.[3] Viewed from this perspective, it is no surprise that new ideas in the social sciences also contributed to the Soviet regime's downfall.

Credit should be given to those social scientists whose conceptions persuaded the new generation of Soviet leaders that democracy would make little difference to their future. If democracy is a sham, as the highest scholarly authorities from Oxford and Harvard maintained, it could be "managed" in the Soviet Union in the same way that it is done in the West. In a similar vein, Gorbachev and his advisers understood the theories of globalism and interdependence as a postmodern version of the old division into spheres of interest, this time by nonmilitary means. The conceptual framework of postcolonial dependency became a positive program for future Soviet relations with the satellite countries.

Very much in the postmodern fashion, Gorbachev's elite viewed limitations imposed by Western democratic structures and international law as a mere smoke screen behind which the center of "real power" resides. Although such a perception was shared by the Soviet elite and postmodern ideologists, they differed substantially in their conclusions. The intellectuals were determined to unmask this power, while the Soviet elite was bent on seizing it. Perhaps that was why Helmut Kohl could so easily convince Gorbachev that between themselves they were creating a postmodern version of the nineteenth-century Concert of Europe, with Germany and Russia taking the leading roles (and, perhaps with the United States, filling the gap left by the Habsburgs).

It is hard to believe that Kohl was sincere. German interests already had surpassed territorial considerations of the kind that preoccupied the Russian leadership. It was the United States rather than Germany that locked into this track of imperial thinking. The first post-Soviet years showed that the Americans expected Russia to become their strategic partner in Eastern Europe, much to the disappointment of other East European peoples. The former dependents of the Soviet Union could not bring themselves to believe that Russia would be able to perform a role in the region similar to the one that the United States has performed in Western Europe—that is, protecting peace and democracy.

To become a postimperial empire, economic and spiritual resources are needed that Russian leaders have found in short supply. Far from being effective in controlling its former colonies, Russia is facing difficulties maintaining territorial integrity within its present borders.

The case for the Russia-first American policy has been presented most clearly by Stephen Shestanovich, who summarized the postcold war settlement in four points: the end of communist government, a stand-down from nuclear confrontation, freedom for Eastern Europe, and the breakup of the USSR.[4] However, the last point, he says, was just a freak accident; nobody intended it. Nonetheless, relations between Russia and other countries of the former Soviet Union have become a test of Russia's intentions toward the rest of the world.

Russia's claim to special relations with "near abroad" is based

on the assurance that a return to ideological or institutional uniformity, typical of the former Soviet Union, is out of the question.
Instead, a wide spectrum of political relationships has been envis-
aged, "neither of full equality nor of outright imperial subordination," representing a mix of political, economic, ethnic, military,
and other ties.[5] Having established such a sphere of influence in
near abroad, Russia no longer would present a danger to Europe.
Shestanovich offers a model of a "degree of influence" that would
be appropriate under the new circumstances. The Russian influence after World War II consisted of three circles of dependence:
the most direct in the Soviet republics; the preponderant in Eastern Europe; and the still significant toward the neutrals, this last
predicament known as Finlandization.

If Russia restored its empire within the borders of the former
Soviet Union, Shestanovich argues, then the countries of the
outer empire—that is, the former satellites—might have feared
Finlandization and rightly so. But if Russia would Finlandize
the former Soviet states, then the former Soviet bloc countries,
much less Western Europe, have nothing to worry about. In other
words, the degree of influence would decrease with geographic
distance. But the geopolitical balance of power may well work in
the opposite direction. The lack of internal consolidation makes
Russia more dependent on geopolitics than is the case with the
better-established states. Russia may exert its influence only by
proximity and within a political vacuum, thus requiring that alternative centers are sufficiently remote or neutralized. It will be
much easier for Russia to subdue Ukraine when that country is
separated from the Western security structures by a "gray area," a
geopolitical vacuum, which is how Henry Kissinger described the
condition of Central Europe following the Soviet Union's demise.

Russia's present position is sometimes compared to that of
France in the 1950s when French withdrawal from NATO caused
great resentment in the United States. A similarity between the
politics of France at that time and Russia today has serious limitations, however. Charles de Gaulle's determination to rid France
of its imperial responsibilities has no analogy among any section

of the Russian political elite, be it reformist, populist, liberal, or, least of all, nationalist. Unlike the French of the 1950s, the Russians today are seeking their lost grandeur simply in recovering at least a "sphere of influence" in the territories of their former empire. And the United States is supposed to help them out by supporting this recovery.

A confusion about where in fact Russia is located has had no precedents in Western Europe this century. Unlike French or British decolonization, the contraction of Russia to its national boundaries is a most ambiguous process. As Richard Pipes has pointed out, it is precisely the difference between the Russian empire and its Western counterparts that the French or British set out to build their empires only after their core states had been relatively well developed, at least administratively. That made it much easier for each country to contract in the aftermath of decolonization.

Whatever the objectives of the present Russian transition, its principal requirement is to have meaningful jurisdiction over a defined territory. That is what Russia seems to lack. The country is still in the course of disintegration, which undercuts the most enlightened projects of reform. And no one knows how to stop it. Possibly it cannot be stopped short of ruthless suppression. If any analogy with France can be made, it would focus on the first years after the French Revolution when regional separatisms encouraged by the disintegration of the old regime were suppressed by Jacobean terror. Two hundred years later, such an option is not feasible.

Helping Russia solve this fundamental difficulty might mean turning a blind eye to a suppression of incipient civil societies taking root in various districts, municipalities, and regions. Since the lack of such local integration has been the crux of Russian internal problems so far, ignoring acts of suppression would not be a right thing to do. It may be that Russia's imperial endurance was possible only in the absence of modern civil societies throughout the vast territories over which it sought domination. It is also possible that a tendency toward disintegration represents a search by the peoples living in those territories for a space that would make representative government a more realistic perspective.

Warsaw in 1993 saw the gesture of remorse made by President Boris Yeltsin, when he bowed before the monument of 20,000 Polish army officers, prisoners of war, murdered in Katyn Forest on Stalin's order in 1940. It was the second great gesture of contrition made by Poland's powerful neighbors. The first was offered in 1969 by Willy Brandt, the chancellor of West Germany, who fell to his knees in front of the monument of the Warsaw Ghetto Rising that marked the last stages of the extermination of Polish Jews. However, a difference exists between the German and Russian acts of remorse.

While the West German government accepted responsibility for the sufferings inflicted on other peoples and asked forgiveness, the Russian president did nothing of the sort. "Democratic Russia cannot be responsible for the deeds of the Soviet leaders," Yeltsin said, "because the Russians were among those who suffered most." Such appears to be the most common attitude among the Russians, regardless of their political affiliations. At the same time, the Russian government is claiming the Soviet heritage wherever it is able to defend it. If the Russians do not feel themselves heirs of the Soviet empire, how can they justify their claims to the territories that never had been in their possession before Stalin annexed them, such as the Kuril Islands or Kaliningrad?

Nobody with a sane mind would suggest revisions of national boundaries in the former Soviet bloc. The examples above only purport to show that it is impossible to pick and choose among entitlements and responsibilities, for they come in a package. One may accept one's inheritance together with debts that come with it, or one can reject both inheritance and debts.

The West German government clearly understood the connection between the best and worst parts of German history, and it accepted both of them. Compensations to the victims of Germany often were misplaced, as were the millions of deutschemarks paid to communist governments while the real victims received next to nothing. But at least there was and still is a sense of responsibility, and an attempt has been made to compensate for past injuries. Nobody expects impoverished Russia to make full financial compensation to victims of the Soviet Union. More important, perhaps, than financial compensation is an admission of moral responsibility for the atrocities committed by the Soviet government on the peoples that fell under its rule. The list is long, and the Russians themselves prominently figure on it.

When Russians are asked, "Who did it?" the most common answer is, "The system did it." But can a system do anything by itself? Next, one will hear that the real culprits were not Russians: Dzerzhinsky was Polish, Stalin was Georgian, Trotsky was Jewish, and so on. Even such a ludicrous line of argument cannot be pursued too far since it was Lenin who handed power to all those baleful foreigners to do what they did. Wasn't Lenin a Russian? Who are the Russians, anyway?

These are questions that Russians cannot escape if they want to continue as a political nation. Other nations, including those that suffered under Soviet rule, can be understanding or even sympathetic to the Russians as they cope with their imperial heritage. Indeed, Russia has so far received more help and sympathy than any other falling empire. It seems, however, as if the Russians' leaders have taken these signs of sympathy as confirmation that their new democratic government may reject any moral responsibility for the Soviet past while taking all the political and territorial advantages that the past bestowed upon them.

Self-inflicted wounds hurt most, but a simple denial is not the way to heal them. The territories of the former Soviet Union harbor the mass graves of millions upon millions who were killed by their own government. The recent resurgence of Stalinist sentiments in Russia is too conspicuous to say that Soviet rulers operated in a social vacuum. With all the problems that have beleaguered Russia, the moral problem is perhaps the most difficult and the most urgent.

Notes

Prologue

1. The quote comes from Gibbon's *Essai,* after D. A. Saunders's introduction to the Penguin Classics edition of *The Decline and Fall of the Roman Empire* (Harmondsworth: 1985), p. 7.

2. Paul Hollander, *Political Pilgrims* (New York: Oxford University Press, 1981). See also Hollander, *Pilgrims on the Run, Encounter* pamphlet no. 16 (1991).

3. Charles Tilly, ed., "Reflections on the History of European State-Making," in *The Formation of National States in Western Europe* (Princeton, N.J.: Princeton University Press, 1975).

1. The First Soviet Generation

1. George Orwell, review of *Power: A New Social Analysis* by Bertrand Russell, *Adelphi,* 1939, in Sonia Orwell and Ian Angus, eds., *The Collected Essays, Journalism, and Letters,* Vol. 1 (London: Penguin Books, 1970), pp. 413-14.

2. Archie Brown, *The Gorbachev Factor* (New York: Oxford University Press, 1996).

3. Valery Boldin, *Ten Years That Shook the World: The Gorbachev Era as Witnessed by His Chief of Staff* (New York: Basic Books, 1994).

4. Zhores Medvedev, *Gorbachev* (Oxford: Blackwell, 1986); Vladimir Solovyov and Elena Klepikova, *Inside the Kremlin* (London: W. H. Allen, 1988).

5. Mikhail Gorbachev, *Perestroika: New Thinking for Our Country and the World* (London: Collins, 1987).

6. Boldin, *Ten Years That Shook the World,* p. 96.

7. Mikhail Gorbachev, *Zhizn i reformy* (Moscow: Novosti, 1995). See also the critical review by the former U.S. ambassador to Moscow, Jack F. Matlock, *New York Review of Books,* 19 December 1996.

8. Boldin, *Ten Years That Shook the World;* Yegor Ligachev, *Inside Gorbachev's Kremlin* (New York: Pantheon, 1993); Eduard Shevardnadze, *The*

Future Belongs to Freedom (New York: Free Press, 1991); A. S. Cheranyev, *Shest let s Gorbachevym: po dnevnikovom zapisam* (Moscow: Kultura, 1993); Nikolai Ryzhkov, *Perestroika: Istoriya predatelstv* (Moscow: Novosti, 1992); Yevgeny Chazov, *Zdrove i vlast: Vospominaniya "Kremlevskogo vracha"* (Moscow: Novosti, 1992); Vadim Medvedev, *V komande Gorbachova* (Moscow: "Bylina," 1994); Andrei Gromyko, *Memoirs* (London: Hutchinson, 1989); Alexander Yakovlev, *Perestroika: nadiezhdy i realnosti* (Moscow: Novosti, 1991).

9. Anatoly Sobchak, *For a New Russia* (London: HarperCollins, 1992); Andrei Sakharov, *Moscow and Beyond, 1986–1989* (New York: Alfred A. Knopf, 1991).

10. Boris Yeltsin, *Against the Grain: An Autobiography* (London: Pan Books, 1990), and *The View from the Kremlin* (London: HarperCollins, 1994).

11. David Remnick, *Lenin's Tomb: The Last Days of the Soviet Empire* (London: Penguin Books, 1994).

12. Ibid., pp. 150–53.

13. David Pryce-Jones, *The War That Never Was: The Fall of the Soviet Empire, 1985–1991* (London: Weidenfeld and Nicolson, 1995).

14. Walter Laqueur, *The Long Road to Freedom: Russia and Glasnost* (New York: Macmillan, 1989).

15. For more detailed analyses of the personnel policy in various periods of Soviet history, see T. H. Rigby, *Political Elites in the USSR: Central Leaders and Local Cadres from Lenin to Gorbachev* (Edward Elgar, England, Vermont 1990); Kenneth C. Farmer, *The Soviet Administrative Elite* (New York: Praeger, 1992); David Lane, "The Soviet Elite: Monolithic or Polyarchic," in Lane, ed., *Russia in Flux* (Aldershot: Edward Elgar, 1992), pp. 3–23; Alexander Rahr, "The Top Leadership: From Soviet Elite to Republican Leadership," in Lane, ed., *Russia in Flux*, pp. 24–37.

16. Jerry F. Hough, *Soviet Leadership in Transition* (Washington, D.C.: Brookings Institution, 1980).

17. Severyn Bialer, *Stalin's Successors: Leadership, Stability, and Change in the Soviet Union* (Cambridge: Cambridge University Press, 1980).

18. For the state of historical sciences in the Soviet Union, see a roundtable discussion in *Kommunist*, no. 12, August 1987. Also Thomas Sherlock, "Politics and History Under Gorbachev," *Problems of Communism*, May–August 1988, pp. 16–42.

19. Laqueur, *The Long Road to Freedom*.

20. *Pravda*, 8 July 1986.

21. *L'Humanité*, 4 February 1986.

22. Interview with Yuri Afanasyev, in Remnick, *Lenin's Tomb*, p. 113.

23. Eduard Shevardnadze, *The Future Belongs to Freedom* (London: Sinclair-Stevenson, 1991).

24. Rigby, *Political Elites*, pp. 260–62.

25. Charles H. Fairbanks, "The Nature of the Beast," *National Interest*, Spring 1993, pp. 46–56.

26. Ibid., p. 53.

27. Interview with Julia Karogodina, in Remnick, *Lenin's Tomb*, pp. 155–58.

28. Remnick, *Lenin's Tomb*, p. 156.

29. Brown, *The Gorbachev Factor*, p. 30.

30. Zhores Medvedev, *Gorbachev*, pp. 38–39; Solovyov and Klepikova, *Inside the Kremlin*, pp. 191–92.

31. Solovyov and Klepikova, *Inside the Kremlin*, pp. 191–92, Brown (*The Gorbachev Factor*, p. 36) presents the story of Gorbachev's aborted internship from a different perspective.

32. See the interview with Zdenek Mlynar, *L'Unita*, 9 April 1985, p. 9.

33. See the interview with Len Karpinsky, in Remnick, *Lenin's Tomb*, pp. 169–75.

34. Solovyov and Klepikova, *Inside the Kremlin*, p. 194.

35. Boldin, *Ten Years That Shook the World*, p. 81.

36. Solovyov and Klepikova, *Inside the Kremlin*, p. 196.

37. Interview with Arkady Volsky, in Remnick, *Lenin's Tomb*, pp. 192.

38. Remnick, *Lenin's Tomb*, p. 518.

39. Interview with Y. Karogodina, in Remnick, *Lenin's Tomb*, p. 156.

40. Interview with Leonid Kravchenko, who was Gorbachev's chief adviser on the use of mass media, in Pryce-Jones, *The War That Never Was*, p. 399.

41. Interview with Valentin Pavlov, in Pryce-Jones, *The War That Never Was*, p. 416.

42. Sobchak, *For a New Russia*, p. 22.

43. Georgy Shakhnazarov, quoted after Brown, *The Gorbachev Factor*, p. 272.

44. Timothy Garton Ash, *In Europe's Name: Germany and the Divided Continent* (London: Jonathan Cape, 1993), p. 118.

45. Boldin, *Ten Years That Shook the World*, p. 85; Brown, *The Gorbachev Factor*, p. 35.

46. Yeltsin, *The View from the Kremlin*, p. 164.

47. Boldin, *Ten Years That Shook the World*, p. 85.

48. J. C. Oates, *New York Times*, 3 January 1988.

49. Interview with Kravchenko, in Pryce-Jones, *The War That Never Was,* p. 399.

50. Ernest Gellner, "Nationalism in the Vacuum," in *Thinking Theoretically about Soviet Nationalisties: History and Comparison in the Study of USSR,* ed. Alexander J. Motyl (New York: Columbia University Press, 1992), pp. 243–55.

51. Interview with Fyodor Burlatsky, in Stephen Cohen and Katarina vanden Heuvel, eds., *Voices of Glasnost: Interviews with Gorbachev's Reformers* (New York: W. W. Norton, 1989).

52. Personal communication with *Progres* editor Victor Gayduk.

53. Fairbanks, "The Nature of the Beast," p. 53.

54. V. Dashishchev, "The Search for New East West Relations," *Literaturnaya Gazeta,* 18 May 1988.

55. Georgy Shakhnazarov, "East-West, The Problem of Deideologizing Relations," *Kommunist,* no. 3, 1989.

56. See, e.g., Andrzej Walicki, *A History of Russian Thought: From the Enlightenment to Marxism* (Oxford: Clarendon Press, 1988).

57. Contrary to what Brown indicates in brackets, the terms "commodity production" and the "law of value" used by Gorbachev in this article derived directly from Marxist rather than market economics.

58. Brown, *The Gorbachev Factor,* p. 224.

59. Ibid., pp. 223–24.

60. Ibid., p. 162.

61. Philip Zelikow and Condolenza Rice, *Germany Unified and Europe Transformed: A Study in Statecraft* (Cambridge, Mass.: Harvard University Press, 1995), p. 276.

62. Hannes Adomeit, "Gorbachev and German Unification," *Problems of Communism,* July–August 1990, p. 15.

63. Shevardnadze, *The Future Belongs to Freedom.*

64. After Alexander Rahr, "The CPSU in the 1980s: Changes in the Party Apparatus," *Journal of Communist Studies,* June 1991, pp. 161–69.

65. Interview with Kravchenko, in Pryce-Jones, *The War That Never Was,* pp. 397–403.

2. Horizontal Disintegration: The Center-Periphery Conflict

1. Nadezhda Mandelstam, *Hope Abandoned* (New York: Atheneum, 1974), p. 285.

2. J. R. Strayer, *On the Medieval Origins of the Modern State* (Princeton,

N.J.: Princeton University Press, 1970), all quotations in this discussion are from p. 69.

3. Arkady Vaksberg, *The Soviet Mafia* (London: Wiedenfeld and Nicolson, 1991).

4. Victor Zaslavsky, "Success and Collapse: Traditional Soviet National Policy," in Jan Bremmer and Ray Taras, eds., *Nations and Politics in the Soviet Successor States* (Cambridge: Cambridge University Press, 1993), pp. 29–42.

5. Victor Zaslavsky, *The Neo-Stalinist State: Class, Ethnicity, and Consensus in Soviet Society*, 2d ed. (Armonk, N.Y.: Sharpe, 1994).

6. Michael Voslensky, *Nomenklatura: Anatomy of the Soviet Ruling Class* (London: The Bodley Head, 1984), p. 377.

7. Victor Zaslavsky, "Nationalism and Democratic Transition in Post-Communist Societies," *Daedalus*, Spring 1992, pp. 97–121.

8. Gregory Khanin, "Economic Growth in the 1980s," in Michael Ellman and Vladimir Kantorovich, eds., *The Disintegration of the Soviet Economic System* (London: Routledge, 1992).

9. Ellman and Kantorovich, eds., *The Disintegration of the Soviet Economic System*.

10. More detailed analyses of these limitations are included in Peter Rutland, *The Myth of the Plan: Lessons of Soviet Planning Experience* (London: Hutchinson, 1985).

11. The proceedings from the conference, "Planning and Management in the National Economy in the COMECON," held by the Polish Academy of Science, Warsaw, INP PAN, 1968.

12. Eugeniusz Zalewski, *Planning Reforms in the Soviet Union, 1962–1966: An Analysis of Recent Trends in Economic Organization and Management* (Chapel Hill: University of North Carolina Press, 1967).

13. G. W. Breslauer, "Is There a Generation Gap in the Soviet Political Establishment? Demand Articulation by RSFSR Provincial Party First Secretaries," *Soviet Studies*, 36, no. 1: 1–25.

14. S. N. Eisenstadt elaborated a broad developmental theory about the fragmentation of highly centralized regimes (which he called pre-bureaucratic) into politically semi-independent units that are capable of an effective resistance to central control. Eisenstadt, *The Political Systems of Empires* (London: Glencoe, 1963).

15. *Peasant Society: A Reader*, ed. Jack M. Potter, May N. Diaz, and George M. Foster (Boston: Little, Brown, 1967).

16. Boris Yeltsin, *Against the Grain* (London: Pan Books, 1991), pp. 54–55.

17. Vaksberg, *The Soviet Mafia*, pp. 111–15.

18. Yegor Ligachev, *Inside Gorbachev's Kremlin* (New York: Pantheon, 1993), p. 123.

19. Alec Nove, *An Economic History of the USSR* (Harmondsworth: Penguin Books, 1986), p. 86.

20. Vladimir Kantorovich, "The Economic Fallacy," *National Interest*, Spring 1993, p. 37.

21. Ibid.

22. Ibid.

23. T. H. Rigby, *Political Elites in the USSR: Central Leaders and Local Cadres from Lenin to Gorbachev*, Edward Elgar, England, Vermont 1990, p. 256, table 11.1.

24. Dawn Mann, "Gorbachev's Personnel Policy: The RSFSR Regional Party First Secretaries," *Report on the USSR*, 10 November 1989.

25. Kantorovich, "The Economic Fallacy," p. 41.

26. V. Borovkin "First Party Secretaries: An Endangered Soviet Species?" *Problems of Communism*, January–February 1990, pp. 15–27.

27. After Alexander Rahr, "The CPSU in the 1980s: Changes in the Party Apparatus," *Journal of Communist Studies*, June 1991, pp. 161–69.

28. Kantorovich, "The Economic Fallacy," p. 42.

29. Max Weber, *Economy and Society* (Berkeley: University of California Press, 1978), pp. 1019–20; C. Tilly, "Reflections on the History of European State-Making," in S. N. Eisenstadt, *The Political Systems of Empires*, pp. 349–52.

30. After Richard Pipes, *Communism: The Vanished Specter* (Oslo: Scandinavian University Press, 1994), p. 32.

31. M. Heller and A. M. Nekrich, *Utopia in Power* (New York: Summit Books, 1986), p. 129.

32. J. A. Getty, *Origins of the Great Purges* (Cambridge: Cambridge University Press, 1985).

33. Antoni Z. Kaminski, "Coercion, Corruption, and Reform: State and Society in the Soviet Type Socialist Regime," *Journal of Theoretical Politics* 1, no. 1 (1989): 77–102.

34. Heller and Nekrich, *Utopia in Power*. Soviet analyst Fyodor Burlatsky also considered Khrushchev's reforms in the territorial party apparatus as the principal cause of his downfall. "Why Khrushchev Failed," *Encounter*, May 1988, p. 31.

35. M. Shafir, "Romania," in Martin McCauley and S. Carter, eds., *Leadership and Succession: The Soviet Union, Eastern Europe, and China* (London: Macmillan, 1986), p. 119; see also M. E. Fisher, "Political Leadership and Personnel Policy in Romania: Continuity and Change,

1965–76," in S. Rosefielde, ed., *World Communism at the Crossroads* (Boston: M. Nijhoff, 1980).

36. J. F. Brown, *Eastern Europe and Communist Rule* (Durham, N.C.: Duke University Press, 1988), p. 243; see also McCauley, "The German Democratic Republic," in McCauley and Carter, eds., *Leadership and Succession*, p. 69.

37. Rigby, *Political Elites in the USRR*, pp. 220–50; Wisła Surazska, "Between Centre and Province: Political Administration in Communist Poland," unpublished thesis, Oxford University, 1990.

38. Ibid., p. 232.

39. For discussion of Polish and Romanian administrative reforms, see D. J. Nelson, "Vertical Integration and Political Control in Eastern Europe: The Polish and Romanian Cases," *Slavic Review* 40, no. 2 (Summer 1981): 210–27.

40. Victoria Bonnel, "Voluntary Associations in Gorbachev's Reform Program," in George Breslauer, ed., *Can Gorbachev's Reform Succeed?* p. 66.

41. John B. Dunlop, *The Rise of Russia and the Fall of the Soviet Empire* (Princeton, N.J.: Princeton University Press, 1993), p. 73.

42. Hélène Carrere d'Encausse, *The End of the Soviet Empire* (New York: Basic Books, 1993), pp. 66–71.

43. Richard Krickus, "Lithuania: Nationalism in the Modern Era," in Bremmer and Taras, *Nations and Politics in the Soviet Successor States*.

44. Richard Pipes, *The Russian Revolution 1899–1919* (London: Collins Harvill, 1990); Leonard Schapiro, *The Communist Party of the Soviet Union*, 2nd ed. (London: Methuen, 1970).

45. John Dunlop, "Russia: Confronting the Loss of Empire," in Bremmer and Taras, eds., *Nations and Politics in the Soviet Successor States*, pp. 43–74.

46. Interview with the speaker of the Supreme Soviet, Anatoly Lukyanov, in David Pryce-Jones, *The War That Never Was: The Fall of the Soviet Empire, 1985–1991* (London: Weidenfeld & Nicolson, 1995), p. 421.

47. Nina Andreyeva, "Ne mogu postupatsa printsipami" (I Cannot Forfeit My Principles), *Sovietskaya Rossiya*, 13 March 1988.

48. The Russian Soviet Federal Socialist Republic (RSFSR), the largest of the fifteen Soviet republics, was the only one without CPSU structures of its own.

3. Vertical Disintegration: The KGB-Military Contest

1. Roman Kolkowicz, *The Soviet Military and the Communist Party* (Princeton, N.J.: Princeton University Press, 1967).

2. See chap. 5 on the party-state relationship.

3. Khrushchev's son, Sergei, suggested that his father's demotion was masterminded by the KGB. However, the military at the least had to give its consent. Sergei Khrushchev, *Khrushchev on Khrushchev* (London: Little, Brown, 1990). Another opinion is that the Khrushchev demise was one of the rare occasions when the KGB and the military cooperated. Victor Suvorov, *Inside the Soviet Army* (London: Grafton Books, 1987).

4. Edward L. Warner, *The Military in Contemporary Soviet Politics* (New York: Praeger, 1977), p. 53.

5. Kolkowicz, *The Soviet Military and the Communist Party*, p. 11.

6. William E. Odom, "The Party-Military Connection: A Critique," in D. R. Herspring and I. Volgyes, eds., *Civil-Military Relations in Communist Systems* (Boulder, Colo.: Westview Press, 1978), pp. 27–52.

7. Suvorov, *Inside the Soviet Army.*

8. Samuel P. Huntington, *The Soldier and the State: The Theory and Politics of Civil-Military Relations* (Cambridge, Mass.: Harvard University Press, 1957).

9. Timothy J. Colton, *Commissars, Commanders, and Civilian Authority: The Structure of Soviet Military Politics* (Cambridge, Mass.: Harvard University Press, 1979).

10. See William Odom's criticism of the interest group interpretation in his "Choice and Change in Soviet Politics," *Problems of Communism,* May–June 1983.

11. Michel Tatu, "Decision Making in the USSR," in Richard Pipes, ed., *Soviet Strategy in Europe* (New York: Crane Russak, 1976), p. 52.

12. Zbigniew Brzezinski, "Soviet Politics: From the Future to the Past?" in Paul Cocks, Robert V. Daniels, and Nancy Whittier Heer, eds., *The Dynamics of Soviet Politics* (Cambridge, Mass.: Harvard University Press, 1976), p. 351.

13. Responsibility for guarding nuclear secrets and weapons installations was left with the KGB. See Amy Knight, "The KGB and Civil-Military Relations," in Timothy J. Colton and T. Gustafson, *Soldiers and the Soviet State: Civil-Military Relations from Brezhnev to Gorbachev* (Princeton, N.J.: Princeton University Press, 1990), p. 252.

14. Michael Voslensky, *Nomenklatura: Anatomy of the Soviet Ruling Class* (London: Bodley Head, 1984), p. 87.

15. Timothy Colton, *Commissars, Commanders, and Civilian Authority.*

16. Some 10 percent of Stalin's generals and colonels began their careers as political commissars. Ibid., p. 96.

17. Ibid.

18. Bruce Parrott, "Political Change and Civil-Military Relations," in Colton and Gustafson, eds., *Soldiers and the Soviet State*, pp. 58–59.

19. Interview with Alexander Yakovlev, in David Remnick, *Lenin's Tomb: The Last Days of the Soviet Empire* (London: Penguin Books, 1994), p. 191.

20. Quoted after Voslensky, *Nomenklatura*, p. 368.

21. *Partiinaia zhizn*, no. 3 (1979): 27; *Kommunist*, no. 10 (1981): 81–82; *Krasnaya Zvezda*, 23 February 1983. For more detailed analysis of Ogarkov's conflict with the civilian Soviet leadership, see Bruce Parrot, "Political Change and Civil-Military Relations," in Colton and Gustafson, eds., *Soldiers and the Soviet State*, pp. 44–92.

22. Andrei Gromyko, *Memoirs* (London: Hutchinson, 1989).

23. Colton and Gustafson, eds., *Soldiers and the Soviet State*, p. 73; Bruce Parrott, "Soviet National Security Under Gorbachev," *Problems of Communism*, November–December 1988, pp. 1–36.

24. Colton and Gustafson, eds., *Soldiers and the Soviet State*, p. 77.

25. According to some commentators, the decision to invade Afghanistan was taken against the better judgment of the military (see P. K. Baev, *The Russian Army in a Time of Trouble* [London: Sage, 1996]), but little evidence supports such an opinion. There is evidence, however, that the army did not want SALT II, and the Afghanistan war put a stop to negotiations on that proposed treaty.

26. Documents used in this chapter come from Mark Kramer, "Poland, 1980–81: Soviet Policy During the Polish Crisis," *Cold War International History Project Bulletin*, Woodrow Wilson International Center for Scholars, Washington, D.C., no. 5 (Spring 1995): 116–139.

27. Rusakov at that time was head of the CC International Department. CPSU CC Politburo transcript, 10 December 1981, in Kramer, "Poland, 1980–81," pp. 135–36.

28. Ryszard Kuklinski, "Wojna z narodem widziana od srodka" (The War with the Nation Seen from the Inside), *Kultura* (Paris), April 1987.

29. M. Wilke, P. Erier, M. Goerner, M. Kubina, and H. P. Muller, *SED-Politburo und polnische Krise 1980/82*, vol. 1: *1980*. Berlin: Forschungsverbund SED-Staat, 1993. After: Kramer, "Poland, 1980–81," pp. 127–28.

30. Kuklinski, "Wojna z narodem widziana od srodka."

31. Ibid.; Kramer, "Poland, 1980–81," p. 136.

32. Kramer, "Poland, 1980–81," p. 123.

33. Jiri Valenta, *Soviet Intervention in Czechoslovakia, 1968* (Baltimore: Johns Hopkins University Press, 1979).

34. Richard D. Anderson, Jr., "Soviet Decision Making and Poland," *Problems of Communism*, March–April 1982, pp. 22–35.

35. *Krasnaya Zvezda*, 16 November 1980.

36. On the December preparations of Soviet forces along the Polish border, see interviews with Czech General Stanislav Prochazka in *Polityka* (Warsaw), 15 September 1990, and *Zemedelske noviny* (Prague), 16 August 1990. See also *Wall Street Journal*, 2 December 1980; *New York Times*, 8 December 1980.

37. Stanislaw Kania, *Zatrzymac Konfrontacje* (Warsaw: BGW, 1991), p. 75.

38. In a series of party conferences conducted in military districts by their new commanders, *Washington Post*, February 13, 1981.

39. Anderson, "Soviet Decision Making and Poland," p. 25, table 1.

40. Ibid.

41. Amy Knight, "The KGB and Civil-Military Relations," in Colton and Gustafson, eds., *Soldiers and the Soviet State*, p. 103.

42. Vaksberg, *The Soviet Mafia*, p. 194.

43. Voslensky, *Nomenklatura*.

44. Yevgeny Chazov, *Zdrove i vlast: Vospominaniya "Kremlovskovo Vracha"* (Health and Power: Rememberings of the Kremlin's Doctor) (Moscow: Novosti, 1992).

45. About this meeting, see Vaksberg, *The Soviet Mafia*, p. 39.

46. Ibid.

47. Jerry F. Hough, "Andropov's First Year," *Problems of Communism*, November-December 1983, pp. 49–64.

48. *Krasnaya Zvezda*, 9 May 1984.

49. Parrott, "Political change and Civil-Military Relations," p. 75.

50. Knight, "The KGB and Civil-Military Relations," pp. 101–2.

51. V. Yasman, "The KGB and Perestroika," *Radio Liberty Research*, 29 August 1988.

52. Charles Fairbanks "The Nature of the Beast," *National Interest*, no. 31 (Spring 1993): 51.

53. Vadim Bakatin, *Izbavlenye of KGB*. (Moscow: Novosti, 1992), p. 37.

54. William E. Odom, "The Soviet Military in Transition," *Problems of Communism*, May-June 1990, p. 58.

55. Parrott, "Political Change and Civil-Military Relations," p. 87.

56. Such a scheme was discussed in several articles in the Soviet press at the time, such as *Literaturnaya Gazeta*, 2 August 1989, and *Literaturnaya Rossiya*, 30 November 1990.

4. The Miracle of German Unification

1. Interview with V. Falin in David Pryce-Jones, *The War That Never Was: The Fall of the Soviet Empire, 1985–1991* (London: Weidenfeld and Nicolson), p. 292.

2. Ibid., p. 291.

3. Interview with Teltschik, in ibid., p. 287.

4. For details on this meeting, see the memoirs of one of the participants, Kohl's adviser, Horst Teltschik, *329 Tage: Innenansichten der Einheit* (Berlin: Wolf Jobst Siedler, 1991).

5. Philip Zelikov and Condolenza Rice, *Germany Unified and Europe Transformed: A Study in Statecraft* (Cambridge, Mass.: Harvard University Press, 1995).

6. Ibid., p. 343.

7. Ibid., pp. 275–79.

8. Ibid., p. 278.

9. Ibid., p. 290.

10. Ibid., p. 348.

11. Ibid., p. 261.

12. Interview with Teltschik, in Pryce-Jones, *The War That Never Was,* p. 286.

13. Timothy Garton Ash, *In Europe's Name: Germany and the Divided Continent* (London: Jonathan Cape, 1993), p. 351.

14. Ibid., pp. 349, 354.

15. Pryce-Jones, *The War That Never Was,* p. 286.

16. Ibid.

17. Ibid.

18. Ash, *In Europe's Name.*

19. Ibid., p. 122.

20. Interview with Falin, in Pryce-Jones, *The War That Never Was,* pp. 288–93.

21. Zelikov and Rice, *Germany Unified and Europe Transformed.*

22. Interview with Alexander Besmertnyk, in Pryce-Jones, *The War That Never Was,* p. 388.

23. Personal communication with one of the participants in this meeting.

24. Bronislaw Geremek, *Rok 1989* (Warsaw: Plejada, 1993), p. 125.

25. Pryce-Jones, *The War That Never Was,* p. 222.

26. Geremek, *Rok 1989,* p. 125.

27. Ibid., p. 124.

28. Ibid., p. 254.

29. Interview with the Hungarian minister of the interior, in Pryce-Jones, *The War That Never Was*, p. 231.

30. Ibid.

31. Ibid. pp. 230–32.

32. Ash, *In Europe's Name*, p. 371; Teltschik, *329 Tage*, p. 35.

33. Pryce-Jones, *The War That Never Was*, p. 284.

34. Ibid.

35. Daniel Johnson, "Last Question," *Spectator*, 2 December 1989.

36. Zelikov and Rice, *Germany Unified and Europe Transformed*.

37. Interview with the commander of the East Berlin military district, in Pryce-Jones, *The War That Never Was*, p. 251.

38. Ibid. p. 252.

39. Ibid. p. 253.

40. Eduard Shevardnadze, *The Future Belongs to Freedom* (London: Sinclair-Stevenson, 1991).

41. Hannes Adomeit, "Gorbachev and German Unification," *Problems of Communism*, July-August, 1990, p. 15.

42. Zelikov and Rice, *Germany Unified and Europe Transformed*, p. 75.

43. Teltchlik, *329 Tage*.

44. Ibid., p. 256.

45. Ash, *In Europe's Name*, p. 355.

46. Pryce-Jones, *The War That Never Was*, p. 284.

47. Personal communication from a member of Gorbachev's staff, Victor Gayduk.

5. Conceptual Revisions

1. Francis Fukuyama, "The Modernizing Imperative," *National Interest*, no. 31 (Spring 1993): 10–18.

2. It originated at the same time as the totalitarian model with Barrington Moore's *Terror and Progress: USSR* (Cambridge, Mass.: Harvard University Press, 1954), and practically dominated studies in the field after the appearance of J. F. Triska and P. M. Cocks, eds., *Political Development in Eastern Europe* (New York: Praeger, 1977).

2. Samuel P. Huntington, *Political Order in Changing Societies* (New Haven, Conn.: Yale University Press, 1968), p. 138.

4. Ibid.

5. Ibid.

6. See the literature on administrative reform in postcommunist countries: Joachim-Jens Hesse, ed., *Administrative Transformation in Central and Eastern Europe: Towards Public Sector Reform in Post-Communist Societies* (Oxford: Blackwell, 1993); Hans-Ulrich Derlien and George Szablowski, eds., "Regime Transition, Elites, and Bureaucracies in Eastern Europe," *Governance* 6, no. 3 (1993).

7. Richard Rose and Yevgeny Tikhomirov, "Who Grows Food in Russia and Eastern Europe?" *Post-Soviet Geography* 34 (February 1993): 117.

8. The survey showed that the great majority of those who grow food in Eastern Europe and Russia (between 50 to 80 percent) are not farmers and that the phenomenon far exceeds a leisure activity. In the Russian cities nearly 30 percent of the inhabitants spend several hours a day on growing their own food, and a further 36 percent tend gardens several times a week. Just 28 percent of inhabitants perform such work only on weekends.

9. Zbigniew Pelczynski, ed., *The State and Civil Society: Studies in Hegel's Political Philosophy* (Cambridge: Cambridge University Press, 1984); Zbigniew Rau, ed., *The Reemergence of Civil Society in Eastern Europe and the Soviet Union* (Boulder, Colo.: Westview Press, 1991); Paul Lewis, ed., *Democracy and Civil Society in Eastern Europe* (New York: St. Martin's Press, 1992).

10. Leonard Binder, "The Crises of Political Development" in Binder et al., *Crises and Sequences in Political Development* (Princeton, N.J.: Princeton University Press, 1971), p. 28.

11. See, for example, Shill's conception of social gaps as typical of underdeveloped societies in his *Political Development in the New States* (New York: Humanities Press, 1962).

12. Jerzy Stempowski, *W Dolinie Dniestru: Listy i Ukrainie* (In the Dniestr Valley: Letters About Ukraine) (Warsaw: LNB, 1992).

13. Antoni Z. Kaminski, *An Institutional Theory of Communist Regimes: Design, Function, and Breakdown* (San Francisco: CS Press, 1992).

14. Personal communication.

15. S. N. Eisenstadt, "The Breakdown of Communist Regimes and the Vicissitudes of Modernity," *Daedalus*, Spring 1992; S. N. Eisenstadt, "Centre-Periphery Relations in the Soviet Empire: Some Interpretative Observations", in A. J. Motyl, ed., *Thinking Theoretically About Soviet Nationalistes. History and Comparison in the Study of USSR* (New York: Columbia University Press, 1992), pp. 205-24.

16. Stefan Nowak, "Jaki ojciec taki syn" (Like Father, Like Son), *Polityka*, 15 March 1980.

17. See, in particular, Seymour Martin Lipset and Stein Rokkan, eds.,

Party Systems and Voter Alignments (New York: Free Press, 1967), pp. 1–63; S. N. Eisenstadt and Stein Rokkan, eds., *Building States and Nations: Models and Data Resources* (London: Sage Publications, 1973).

18. Stein Rokkan, "Geography, Religion and Social Class: Crosscutting Cleavages in Norwegian Politics," in Lipset and Rokkan, eds., *Party Systems and Voter Alignments*, pp. 367–444; see also "Nation Building, Cleavage Formation, and the Structuring of Mass Politics," in Stein Rokkan, A. Campbell, P. Torsvik, and H. Valen, *Citizens, Elections, Parties: Approaches to the Comparative Study of the Process of Development* (Oslo: Universitetsforlaget, 1970), pp. 72–144.

19. K. C. Martis, Z. Kovacs, D. Kovacs, and D. S. Peter, "The Geography of the 1990 Hungarian Parliamentary Elections" *Political Geography* 11, no. 3 (May 1992): 283–305; Andrej Florczyk and Tomasz Zukowski, "Nowa Geografia Polityczna Polski," in Lena Kolarska-Bobinska, Pawel Lukasiewicz, and Zbigniew W. Rykowski, eds., *Wyniki Badan—Wyniki Wyborow 4 Czerwca 1989* (Warsaw: Polish Sociological Society, 1990); T. Kostelecki, "Volby '92 v Ceske republice ocima geografa: zadna velka prekvapeni," *Geograficke rozhledy*, no. 1 (1992–93): 4–6.

20. Jadwiga Staniszkis, *The Dynamics of the Breakthrough in Eastern Europe: The Polish Experience* (Berkeley: University of California Press, 1991).

21. *La dottrina del Fascismo*, published under Mussolini's name but written by Giovanni Gentille.

22. "For the fascist everything is within the State and neither individual nor groups are outside the state. For Fascism the state is an absolute, before which individuals and groups are only relative." Ibid.

23. Hannah Arendt, *The Origins of Totalitarianism* (London: Andre Deutsch, 1986 [1951]).

24. More exactly, the totalitarian syndrome suggested by Carl Friedrich and Zbigniew Brzezinski consisted of an official ideology, a single mass party usually led by a charismatic leader, central monopoly over a means of coercion as well as over mass communication and economy, and terroristic police control. Carl J. Friedrich and Zbigniew K. Brzezinski, *Totalitarian Dictatorship and Autocracy* (Cambridge, Mass.: Harvard University Press, 1965).

25. Arendt, *The Origins of Totalitarianism*, p. 257.

26. Robert C. Tucker, *Political Culture and Leadership in Soviet Russia: From Lenin to Gorbachev* (New York: Norton, 1987).

27. M. Broszat, *The Hitler State* (New York: Longman, 1987).

28. Juan J. Linz, "Totalitarian and Authoritarian Regimes," in Fred J.

Greenstein and Nelson W. Polsby, eds., *Handbook of Political Science,* vol. 3 (Reading, Mass.: Addison-Wesley, 1976), p. 212.

29. Jeane J. Kirkpatrick, "Dictatorships and Double Standards," *Commentary,* November 1979.

30. Ernest Fraenkel, *The Dual State: A Contribution to the Theory of Dictatorship* (New York: Free Press, 1947).

31. Ibid.

32. See also some other versions of totalitarian models suggested by these authors in Zbigniew Brzezinski, *Ideology and Power in Soviet Politics* (New York: Praeger, 1962); and Carl Friedrich, "The Evolving Theory and Practice of Totalitarian Regimes," in Carl J. Friedrich, Michael Curtis, and Benjamin R. Barber, eds., *Totalitarianism in Perspective: Three Views* (New York: Praeger, 1969).

33. Here is Mussolini's own confession to his friend: "If you could only imagine the effort which it has cost me to search for some kind of equilibrium in which the collisions could be avoided between the antagonistic powers which jostle each other—all jealous and distrustful of one another: the government, the party, the monarchy, the Vatican, the army, the militia, the prefects, the ministers, the big monopoly interests. You will understand, my good friend, these things are the indigestion of totalitarianism." After Leonard Schapiro, *Totalitarianism* (London: Pall Mall Press, 1972), p. 26.

34. Some other totalitarian features were suggested, such as a drive toward world domination, the subjugation of legal order, control of private morality, and others. Schapiro, *Totalitarianism.*

35. Stanislav Andreski, *Max Weber's Insights and Errors* (London: Routledge & Kegan Paul, 1984).

36. Max Weber, *Essays in Sociology,* ed. H. H. Gerth and C. Wright Mills (New York: Oxford University Press, 1958).

37. See, for example, David Lane, *The End of Social Inequality?* (London: Allen and Unwin, 1982); Marian Sawer, ed., *Socialism and the New Class,* APSA Monograph no. 19, Adelaide, 1978; Milovan Djilas, *The New Class: An Analysis of the Communist System* (New York: Holt, Reinhart, and Winston, 1946); Voslensky, *Nomenklatura.*

38. On this point, see Jan Pakulski, "Bureaucracy as the Soviet System," *Studies in Comparative Communism,* no. 1 (Spring 1986): 3–24.

39. A. Mayer, "The Comparative Study of Communist Political Systems," in Richard Cornell, ed., *The Soviet Political System* (Englewood Cliffs, N.J.: Prentice-Hall, 1970), p. 48.

40. For example, Jadwiga Staniszkis, *Patologie Struktur Organizacyjnych*

(The Pathology of Organizational Structures) (Warsaw: Polska Akademia Nauk, Instytut Filizofii i Socjologii, 1972).

41. Paul Hollander, "Observations on bureaucracy, totalitarianism and the Comparative Study of Communism," in Cornell, ed., *The Soviet Political System*, p. 48.

42. Patrimonial bureaucracy was described by Weber as a mixture of modern and traditional elements. It consisted of "hierarchical organisation with impersonal spheres of competence, but occupied by unfree officials" and therefore compatible with the system of personal domination. Moreover, Weber distinguished the "prebendal" form of bureaucratic administration where "remuneration takes a form of revenues from property allocated for life." None of these forms is compatible with the formal-rational bureaucracy which is contractual and paid in money. Weber, *Economy and Society*, pp. 220–21.

43. R. Bendix, *Max Weber: An Intellectual Portrait* (Berkeley: University of California Press, 1977), pp. 465–66.

44. Aryeh L. Unger, *Constitutional Development in the USSR: A Guide to the Soviet Constitutions* (London: Methuen, 1981), pp. 277–80.

45. For a discussion on institutionalization in communist societies, see Graeme Gill, "Institutionalization and Revolution: Rules and the Soviet Political System," *Soviet Studies* 37, no. 2 (1985): 212–26, followed by polemic between Gill and Malley, in *Soviet Studies* 38, no. 1 (January 1986): 103–7.

46. Ernest Gellner, *Plough, Sword, and Book: The Structure of Human History* (London: Grafton Books, 1991), p. 215.

47. Surazska, *Between Centre and Province*, pp. 104–44.

48. Unger, *Constitutional Development in the USSR*, p. 79.

49. For Khrushchev's secret speech to the Twentieth Congress of the CPSU, see the English version, Nikita S. Khrushchev, *Khrushchev Remembers* (Boston: Little, Brown, 1970), pp. 559–618.

50. T. Lowitt, "Le parti polymorphe en Europe de l'Est," *Revue française de science politique* 24, no. 4/5 (September/October, 1979).

51. Richard Bendix, *Max Weber*, p. 467.

52. Merle Fainsod, *How Russia Is Ruled*, 2nd ed. (Cambridge, Mass.: Harvard University Press, 1963), p. 388.

53. Weber listed the following tactics typically applied by arbitrary rulers: brief terms of territorial officials; the exclusion of officials from districts with which they had been previously associated; the system of spying, reporting, and supervision by official overseers occasionally sent from the center; empowering officials from case to case without estab-

lishing any consistent division of labor; setting apart the group of officials from the rest of society so as to make them dependent on the center, etc. Weber, *Economy. . .* , p. 1043.

54. About the same paradox under patrimonial regimes, see ibid., pp. 1019–20.

55. J. J. Wiatr and A. Przeworski, "Control Without Opposition," *Government and Opposition* 1, no. 2 (1966).

56. *Z Zagadnien Teorii i Praktyki Funkcjonowania Partii* (Issues on the Theory and Practice of the Functioning of the Party) (Warsaw: The Higher School of Social Sciences at the CC PZPR, 1971).

57. Ibid., p. 369.

58. Kenneth Jowitt, *Leninist Response to National Dependency* (Berkeley: University of California, Institute of International Studies, 1978), p. 34.

59. Bendix, *Max Weber,* p. 2.

60. Richard Bendix, *Work and Authority in Industry* (Berkeley: University of California Press, 1974), p. xl.

61. R. L. Satow, "Value-Rational Authority and Professional Organizations: Weber's Missing Type," *Administrative Science Quarterly* 20 (December 1975): 526–31; T. H. Rigby, "Introduction," in Rigby and F. Feher, eds., *Political Legitimization in Communist States* (London: Macmillan, 1982), p. 12; Pakulski, "Bureaucracy as the Soviet System."

62. Max Weber, *Economy and Society,* vol. 1 (Berkeley: University of California Press, 1978), pp. 111, 284; see also Weber's "Socialism" in W. G. Runciman, ed., *Selection in Translations* (Cambridge: Cambridge University Press, 1978), pp. 251–62.

6. Despotism and the Modern State

1. Max Weber, *The Theory of Social and Economic Organization* (New York: Oxford University Press, 1947), p. 413.

2. Montesquieu, *The Spirit of the Laws,* trans. Thomas Nugent, vol. 1 (Cincinnati: Robert Clarke, 1886), p. 213.

3. For a discussion of such double roles of the state, see, for example, Guillermo O'Donnell, "Tensions in the Bureaucratic-Authoritarian State and the Question of Democracy," in D. Collier, ed., *The New Authoritarianism* (Princeton, N.J.: Princeton University Press, 1979).

4. T. H. Rigby, *Lenin's Government: Sovnarkom 1917–1922* (Cambridge: Cambridge University Press, 1979).

5. Neil Harding, "Socialism, Society, and the Organic Labor State," in

Harding, ed., *The State in Socialist Society* (London: Macmillan, 1984), pp. 1–50.

6. Karl Marx, "Address of the General Council of the International Working Men's Association," in E. Kamenka, ed., *The Portable Karl Marx* (Harmondsworth: Penguin Books, 1985), p. 517.

7. Rigby, *Lenin's Government*, pp. 10–40.

8. This was one of Friedrich A. Hayek's arguments against central planning; see *The Road to Serfdom* (London: Routledge and Kegan Paul, 1986), pp. 42–54.

9. Carl Schmitt, *Political Theology: Four Chapters on the Concept of Sovereignty* (Cambridge, Mass.: MIT Press, 1985).

10. Ibid., p. 26.

11. Aleksandr Tsipko, "Khoroshi li nashi printsipy?" (Are Our Principles Any Good?) *Novyi mir,* no. 4 (1990): 173-204.

Epilogue

1. Carl J. Friedrich, *Constitutional Government and Democracy* (Boston: Little, Brown, 1946).

2. Henry Kissinger, *Diplomacy* (New York: Simon and Schuster, 1994), p. 141.

3. Ernest Gellner, *Plough, Sword, and Book: The Structure of Human History* (London: Grafton Books, 1991), p. 216.

4. Stephen Shestanovich, "Giving Russia Its Due," *National Interest,* Summer 1994.

5. Ibid.

Bibliography

Adomeit, Hannes. "Gorbachev and German Unification." *Problems of Communism*, July–August 1990.

Anderson, R. D., Jr. "Soviet Decision Making and Poland." *Problems of Communism*, March–April 1982, pp. 22–35.

Andreski, Stanislav. *Max Weber's Insights and Errors*. London: Routledge & Kegan Paul, 1984.

Arendt, Hannah. *The Origins of Totalitarianism*, London: André Deutsch, 1986 [1951].

Ash, Timothy Garton. *In Europe's Name: Germany and the Divided Continent*. London: Jonathan Cape, 1993.

Baev, P. K. *The Russian Army in a Time of Trouble*. London: Sage, 1996.

Bakatin, Vadim. *Izbavlenye of KGB*. Moscow: Novosti, 1992.

Bendix, R. *Max Weber: An Intellectual Portrait*. Berkeley: University of California Press, 1977.

————. *Work and Authority in Industry*. Berkeley: University of California Press, 1974.

Bialer, Severyn. *Stalin's Successors: Leadership, Stability, and Change in the Soviet Union*. Cambridge: Cambridge University Press, 1980.

Binder, Leonard. "The Crises of Political Development," in L. Binder, J. D. Coleman, J. La Palombara, L. W. Pye, S. Verba, and M. Weiner, *Crises and Sequences in Political Development*, pp. 3–72. Princeton, N.J.: Princeton University Press, 1971.

Boldin, Valery. *Ten Years That Shook the World: The Gorbachev Era as Witnessed by His Chief of Staff*. New York: Basic Books, 1994.

Bonnel, V. "Voluntary Associations in Gorbachev's Reform Program," in George Breslauer, ed., *Can Gorbachev's Reform Succeed?* Berkeley: University of California, 1990.

Borovkin, V. "First Party Secretaries: An Endangered Soviet Species?" *Problems of Communism*, January–February 1990, pp. 15–27.

Breslauer, George. *Can Gorbachev's Reform Succeed?* Berkeley: University of California Press, 1990.

————. "Is There a Generation Gap in the Soviet Political Establishment? Demand Articulation by RSFSR Provincial Party First Secretaries." *Soviet Studies* 36, no. 1: 1–25.

Broszat, Martin. *The Hitler State.* New York: Longman, 1987.

Brown, Archie. *The Gorbachev Factor.* Oxford: Oxford University Press, 1996.

Brown, J. F. *Eastern Europe and Communist Rule.* Durham, N.C.: Duke University Press, 1988.

Brzezinski, Zbigniew. *Ideology and Power in Soviet Politics.* New York: Praeger, 1962.

———. "Soviet Politics: From the Future to the Past?" in Paul Cocks, Richard V. Daniels, and Nancy Whittier Heer, eds., *The Dynamics of Soviet Politics.* Cambridge, Mass.: Harvard University Press, 1976. Pp. 337–51.

Burlatsky, Fyodor. "Why Khrushchev Failed." *Encounter,* May 1988.

Carrère d'Encausse, Hélène. *The End of the Soviet Empire.* New York: Basic Books, 1993.

Chazov, Yevgeny. *Zdrove i vlast: Vospominaniya "Kremlevskogo vracha."* Moscow: Novosti, 1992.

Cheranyev, A. S. *Shest let s Gorbachevym: po dnevnikovom zapisam.* Moscow: Kultura, 1993.

Cocks, Paul, Robert V. Daniels, Nancy Whittier Heer, eds. *The Dynamics of Soviet Politics.* Cambridge, Mass.: Harvard University Press, 1976.

Cohen, Stephen F., and Katrina vanden Heuvel. *Voices of Glasnost: Conversations with Gorbachev's Reformers.* New York: W. W. Norton, 1989.

Colton, Timothy J. *Commissars, Commanders, and Civilian Authority: The Structure of Soviet Military Politics.* Cambridge, Mass.: Harvard University Press, 1979.

Colton, Timothy J., and Gustafson Tane. *Soldiers and the Soviet State: Civil-Military Relations from Brezhnev to Gorbachev.* Princeton, N.J.: Princeton University Press, 1990.

COMECON. *Planning and Management in the National Economy in the COMECON.* Proceedings from the conference, Warsaw: INP PAN, 1968.

Derlien, H. U., and G. Szablowski, eds. *Regime Transition, Elites, and Bureaucracies in Eastern Europe. Governance* 6, no. 3 (1993).

Djilas, Milovan. *The New Class: An Analysis of the Communist System.* New York, London; Holt, Rinehart and Winston, 1957.

Dunlop, J. B. *The Rise of Russia and the Fall of the Soviet Empire.* Princeton, N.J.: Princeton University Press, 1993.

———. "Russia: Confronting the Loss of Empire," in J. Bremmer and R. Taras, eds., *National Politics in the Soviet Successor States.* Cambridge: Cambridge University Press, 1993.

Eisenstadt, S. N. "The Breakdown of Communist Regimes and the Vicissitudes of Modernity." *Daedalus,* Spring 1992.

―――. "Centre-Periphery Relations in the Soviet Empire: Some Interpretative Observations," in A. J. Motyl, ed., *Thinking Theoretically about Soviet Nationalisties: History and Comparison in the Study of USSR.* New York: Columbia University Press, 1992. Pp. 205–24.

―――. *The Political Systems of Empires.* London: Glencoe, 1963.

Eisenstadt, S. N., and Stein Rokkan, eds. *Building States and Nations: Models and Data Resources.* London: Sage Publications, 1973.

Ellman, Michael, and Vladimir Kantorovich, eds. *The Disintegration of the Soviet Economic System.* London: Routledge, 1992.

Fainsod, Merle. *How Russia Is Ruled.* 2nd ed. Cambridge, Mass.: Harvard University Press, 1963.

Fairbanks, Charles H. "The Nature of the Beast." *National Interest,* Spring 1993, pp. 46–56.

Farmer, Kenneth C. *The Soviet Administrative Elite.* New York: Praeger, 1992.

Fisher, M. E. "Political Leadership and Personnel Policy in Romania: Continuity and Change, 1965–76," in S. Rosefielde, ed., *World Communism at the Crossroads.* Boston: M. Nijhoff, 1980.

Florczyk, A., and T. Zukowski. "Nowa Geografia Polityczna Polski," in L. Kolarska-Bobinska, P. Lukasiewicz, and Z. W. Rykowski, eds., *Wyniki Badan—Wyniki Wyborow 4 Czerwca 1989.* Warsaw: Polish Sociological Society, 1990.

Foster, G. M. "Peasant Society and the Image of the Limited Good," in J. M. Potter, M. N. Diaz, and G. M. Foster, eds., *Peasant Society: A Reader.* Boston: Little, Brown, 1967.

Fraenkel, Ernest. *The Dual State: A Contribution to the Theory of Dictatorship.* New York: Free Press, 1947.

Friedrich, Carl J. *Constitutional Government and Democracy.* Boston: Little, Brown, 1946.

―――. "The Evolving Theory and Practice of Totalitarian Regimes," in Friedrich, L. Curtis, and B. Barber, eds., *Totalitarianism in Perspective: Three Views.* London: 1969.

Friedrich, Carl J. and Zbigniew K. Brzezinski. *Totalitarian Dictatorship and Autocracy.* Cambridge, Mass.: Harvard University Press, 1965.

Friedrich, Carl J., Michael Curtis, and B. R. Barber. *Totalitarianism in Perspective: Three Views.* New York: Praeger, 1969.

Fukuyama, Francis. The Modernizing Imperative," *National Interest,* no. 31 (Spring 1993): 10–18.

Gellner, Ernest. "Nationalism in the Vacuum," in Alexander J. Motyl, ed., *Thinking Theoretically about Soviet Nationalisties: History and Comparison in the Study of USSR*. New York: Columbia University Press, 1992. Pp. 243–55.

———. *Plough, Sword, and Book: The Structure of Human History*. London: Paladin Grafton, 1991.

Geremek, B. *Rok 1989*. Warsaw: Plejada, 1993.

Getty, J. Arch. *Origins of the Great Purges*. Cambridge: Cambridge University Press, 1985.

Gibbon, Edward. *The History of the Decline and Fall of the Roman Empire*. London: Penguin Classics, 1985.

Gill, Graeme. "Institutionalization and Revolution: Rules and the Soviet Political System." *Soviet Studies* 37, no. 2 (1985): 212–26.

Gorbachev, Mikhail. *Perestroika: New Thinking for Our Country and the World*. London: Collins, 1987.

———. *Zhizn i reformy*. Moscow: Novosti, 1995.

Greenstein, F. I., and N. W. Polsby, eds. *Handbook of Political Science*. Reading, Mass.: Addison-Wesley, 1976.

Gromyko, Andrei. *Memoirs*. London: Hutchinson, 1989.

Harding, Neil. "Socialism, Society, and the Organic Labor State," in N. Harding, ed., *The State in Socialist Society*. London: Macmillan, 1984. Pp. 1–50.

Hayek, Friedrich A. *The Road to Serfdom*. London: Routledge and Kegan Paul, 1986.

Heller, M., and Nekrich, A. M. *Utopia in Power*. New York: Summit Books, 1986.

Hesse, J. J., ed. *Administrative Transformation in Central and Eastern Europe: Towards Public Sector Reform in Post-Communist Societies*. Oxford: Blackwell, 1993.

Hollander, Paul. "Observations on Bureaucracy, Totalitarianism, and the Comparative Study of Communism," in R. Cornell, ed., *The Soviet Political System*. Englewood Cliffs, N.J.: Prentice-Hall, 1970.

———. *Pilgrims on the Run*. *Encounter* pamphlet no. 16 (1991).

———. *Political Pilgrims*. New York: Oxford University Press, 1981.

Hough, Jerry F. "Andropov's First Year." *Problems of Communism*, November-December 1983, pp. 49–64.

———. *Soviet Leadership in Transition*. Washington, D.C.: Brookings Institution, 1980.

Huntington, Samuel P. *Political Order in Changing Societies*. New Haven, Conn.: Yale University Press, 1968.

———. *The Soldier and the State: The Theory and Politics of Civil-Military Relations.* Cambridge, Mass.: Harvard University Press, 1957.

Jowitt, Kenneth. *Leninist Response to National Dependency.* Berkeley: University of California, Institute of International Studies, 1978.

Kaminski, A. Z. "Coercion, Corruption, and Reform: State and Society in the Soviet Type Socialist Regime." *Journal of Theoretical Politics* 1, no. 1 (1989): 77–102.

———. *An Institutional Theory of Communist Regimes: Design, Function, and Breakdown.* San Francisco: CS Press, 1992.

Kania, S. *Zatrzymac Konfrontacje,* Warsaw: BGW, 1991.

Kantorovich, V. "The Economic Fallacy." *National Interest,* Spring 1993, pp. 35–45.

Khanin, Gregory. "Economic Growth in the 1980s," in Michael Ellman and Vladimir Kantorovich, eds., *The Disintegration of the Soviet Economic System.* London: Routledge, 1992.

Khrushchev, Nikita S. *Khrushchev Remembers.* Boston: Little, Brown, 1970.

Kirkpatrick, J. J. "Dictatorships and Double Standards." *Commentary,* November, 1979.

Kissinger, Henry. *Diplomacy.* New York: Simon & Schuster, 1994.

Knight, Amy W. "The KGB and Civil-Military Relations," in Timothy J. Colton, and T. Gustafson, eds., *Soldiers and the Soviet State: Civil-Military Relations from Brezhnev to Gorbachev.* Princeton, N.J.: Princeton University Press, 1990.

Kolkowicz, Roman. *The Soviet Military and the Communist Party.* Princeton, N.J.: Princeton University Press, 1967.

Kostelecki, T. "Volby '92 v Ceske republice ocima geografa: zadna velka prekvapeni." *Geograficke rozhledy,* no. 1 (1992–93): 4–6.

Kramer, Mark. "Poland, 1980–81; Soviet Policy During the Polish Crisis," *Cold War International History Project Bulletin,* issue 5 (Spring 1995): 116–39. Woodrow Wilson International Center for Scholars, Washington, D.C.

Krickus, R. "Lithuania: Nationalism in the Modern Era," in Ian Bremmer and Ray Taras, eds., *Nation and Politics in the Soviet Successor States.* Cambridge: Cambridge University Press, 1993.

Krygier, M. "Bureaucracy in Trotsky's Analysis of Stalinism," in Marian Sawer, ed., *Socialism and the New Class.* Adelaide, South Australia: APSA Monograph 19, 1978.

Kuklinski, R. "Wojna z narodem widziana od srodka" (The War with the Nation Seen from the Inside). *Kultura* (Paris), April 1987.

Lane, David. *The End of Social Inequality?* London: Allen and Unwin, 1982.

———. "The Soviet Elite: Monolithic or Polyarchic." In Lane, ed., *Russia in Flux.* Aldershot: Edward Elgar, 1992.

Laqueur, Walter. *The Long Road to Freedom: Russia and Glasnost.* New York: Macmillan, 1989.

Lewis, Paul, ed. *Democracy and Civil Society in Eastern Europe.* New York: St. Martin's Press, 1992.

Ligachev, Yegor. *Inside Gorbachev's Kremlin.* New York: Pantheon, 1993.

Linz, Juan J. "Totalitarian and Authoritarian Regimes," in Fred J. Greenstein and Nelson W. Polsby, eds., *Handbook of Political Science,* vol. 3.

Lipset, Seymour Martin, and Stein Rokkan, eds., *Party Systems and Voter Alignments.* New York: Free Press, 1967. Pp. 1–63.

Lowitt, T. "Le parti polymorphe en Europe de l'Est." *Revue française de science politique* 24, no. 4/5 (September-October, 1979).

McCauley, Martin, and Stephen Carter, eds. *Leadership and Succession: The Soviet Union, Western Europe, and China.* London: Macmillan, 1986.

Mandelstam, Nadezhda. *Hope Abandoned.* New York: Atheneum, 1974.

Mann, D. "Gorbachev's Personnel Policy: The RSFSR Regional Party First Secretaries." *Report on the USSR,* November 10, 1989.

Martis, K. C., Z. Kovacs, D. Kovacs, and S. Peter. "The Geography of the 1990 Hungarian Parliamentary Elections." *Political Geography* 11, no. 3 (May 1992): 283–305.

Marx, Karl. "Address of the General Council of the International Working Men's Association," in E. Kamenka, ed., *The Portable Karl Marx.* Harmondsworth: Penguin Books, 1985. P. 517.

Mayer, A. "The Comparative Study of Communist Political Systems," in Richard Cornell, ed., *The Soviet Political System.* Englewood Cliffs, N.J.: Prentice-Hall, 1970.

Medvedev, Vadim. *V komande Gorbachova.* Moscow: "Bylina," 1994.

Medvedev, Zhores. *Gorbachev.* Oxford: Blackwell, 1986.

Montesquieu, Charles Louis. *The Spirit of the Laws,* trans. Thomas Nugent. Vol. 1. Cincinnati: Robert Clarke, 1886.

Nelson, D. J. "Vertical Integration and Political Control in Eastern Europe: The Polish and Romanian Cases." *Slavic Review* 40, no. 2 (Summer 1981).

Nove, Alec. *An Economic History of the USSR.* Harmondsworth: Penguin Books, 1986.

Odom, W. E. "Choice and Change in Soviet Politics." *Problems of Communism,* May–June 1983.

———. "The Party-Military Connection: A Critique," in D. R. Herspring and I. Volgyes, eds., *Civil-Military Relations in Communist Systems*. Boulder, Colo.: Westview Press, 1978.

———. "The Soviet Military in Transition." *Problems of Communism*, May–June 1990.

O'Donnell, Guillermo. "Tensions in the Bureaucratic-Authoritarian State and the Question of Democracy," in D. Collier, ed., *The New Authoritarianism*. Princeton, N.J.: Princeton University Press, 1979.

Orwell, George. *After: The Collected Essays, Journalism, and Letters*, ed. Sonia Orwell and Ian Angus. Vol. 1. London: Penguin Books, 1970.

Pakulski, Jan. "Bureaucracy as the Soviet System." *Studies in Comparative Communism*, no. 1 (Spring 1986): 3–24.

Parrott, Bruce. "Political Change and Civil-Military Relations," in Timothy J. Colton and Thane Gustafson, eds., *Soldiers and the Soviet State: Civil-Military Relations from Brezhnev to Gorbachev*. Princeton, N.J.: Princeton University Press, 1990.

———. "Soviet National Security Under Gorbachev." *Problems of Communism*, November–December 1988, pp. 1–36.

Pelczynski, Z. A., ed. *The State and Civil Society: Studies in Hegel's Political Philosophy*. Cambridge: Cambridge University Press, 1984.

Pipes, Richard. *Communism: The Vanished Specter*. Scandinavian University Press, 1994.

———. *The Russian Revolution 1899–1919*. London: Collins Harvill, 1990.

———, ed. *Soviet Strategy in Europe*. New York: Crane Russak, 1976.

Potter, Jack, May N. Diaz, and George M. Foster, eds. *Peasant Society: A Reader*. Boston: Little, Brown, 1967.

Pryce-Jones, David. *The War That Never Was: The Fall of the Soviet Empire, 1985–1991*. London: Weidenfeld & Nicolson, 1995.

Rahr, Alexander. "The CPSU in the 1980s: Changes in the Party Apparatus." *Journal of Communist Studies*, June 1991, pp. 161–69.

———. "The Top Leadership: From Soviet Elite to Republican Leadership," in David Lane, ed., *Russia in Flux*. Aldershot: Edward Elgar, 1992.

Rau, Zbigniew, ed. *The Reemergence of Civil Society in Eastern Europe and the Soviet Union*. Boulder, Colo.: Westview Press, 1991.

Remnick, David. *Lenin's Tomb: The Last Days of the Soviet Empire*. London: Penguin Books, 1994.

Rigby, T. H. *Lenin's Government: Sovnarkom, 1917–1922*. Cambridge: Cambridge University Press, 1979.

———. *Political Elites in the USSR: Central Leaders and Local Cadres from Lenin to Gorbachev*. Vermont: Edward Elgar, 1990.

Rigby, T. H., and Ferenc Fehér, eds. *Political Legitimization in Communist States*. London: Macmillan, 1982.

Rokkan, Stein. "Geography, Religion, and Social Class: Crosscutting Cleavages in Norwegian Politics," in Seymour Martin Lipset and Stein Rokkan, eds., *Party Systems and Voter Alignments*. New York: Free Press, 1967. Pp. 367–444.

Rokkan, Stein, A. Campbell, P. Torsvik, and H. Valen. *Citizens, Elections, Parties: Approaches to the Comparative Study of the Process of Development*. Oslo: Universitetsforlaget, 1970.

Rose, R., and Y. Tikhomirov. "Who Grows Food in Russia and Eastern Europe?" *Post-Soviet Geography* 34 (February 1993).

Rutland, Peter. *The Myth of the Plan: Lessons of Soviet Planning Experience*. London: Hutchinson, 1985.

Ryzhkov, Nikolai. *Perestroika: Istoriya predatelstv*. Moscow: Novosti, 1992.

Sakharov, Andrei. *Moscow and Beyond, 1986–1989*. New York: Alfred A. Knopf, 1991.

Satow, R. L. "Value-Rational Authority and Professional Organisations: Weber's Missing Type." *Administrative Science Quarterly* 20 (December 1975): 526–31.

Schapiro, Leonard. *The Communist Party of the Soviet Union*. 2nd ed. London: Methuen, 1970.

———. *Totalitarianism*. London: Pall Mall Press, 1972.

Schmitt, Carl. *Political Theology: Four Chapters on the Concept of Sovereignty*. Cambridge, Mass.: MIT Press, 1985.

Sherlock, Thomas. "Politics and History Under Gorbachev." *Problems of Communism*, May–August 1988, pp. 16–42.

Shevardnadze, Eduard. *The Future Belongs to Freedom*. London: Sinclair-Stevenson, 1991.

Shill, S. *Political Development in the New States*. New York: Humanities Press, 1962.

Sobchak, Anatoly. *For a New Russia*. London: HarperCollins, 1992.

Solovyov, Vladimir, and Elena Klepikova. *Inside the Kremlin*. London: W. H. Allen, 1988.

Staniszkis, Jadwiga. *The Dynamics of the Breakthrough in Eastern Europe: The Polish Experience*. Berkeley: University of California Press, 1991.

———. *Patologie Struktur Organizacyjnych* (The Pathology of Organizational Structures). Warsaw: Polska Akademia Nauk, Instytut Filizofii i Socjologii, 1972.

Stempowski, J. *W Dolinie Dniestru: Listy i Ukrainie* (In the Dniestr Valley: Letters About Ukraine). Warsaw: LNB, 1992.

Strayer, J. R. *On the Medieval Origins of the Modern State.* Princeton, N.J.: Princeton University Press, 1970.

Surazska, Wisła. "Between Centre and Province: Political Administration in Communist Poland." Unpublished thesis, Oxford University, 1990.

Suvorov, Viktor. *Inside the Soviet Army.* London: Grafton Books, 1987.

Shestanovich, S. "Giving Russia Its Due." *National Interest,* Summer 1994.

Tatu, Michel. "Decision Making in the USSR," in Richard Pipes, ed., *Soviet Strategy in Europe.* New York: Crane Russak, 1976. Pp. 45–64.

Teltschik, Horst. *329 Tage: Innenansichten der Einheit.* Berlin: Wolf Jobst Siedler, 1991.

Tilly, Charles, ed. *The Formation of National States in Western Europe.* Princeton, N.J.: Princeton University Press, 1975.

Triska, J. F., and P. M. Cocks, eds. *Political Development in Eastern Europe.* New York: Praeger, 1977.

Unger, Aryeh L. *Constitutional Development in the USSR: A Guide to the Soviet Constitutions.* London: Methuen, 1981.

Vaksberg, Arkady. *The Soviet Mafia.* London: Weidenfeld and Nicolson, 1991.

Valenta, Jiri. *Soviet Intervention in Czechoslovakia, 1968.* Baltimore: Johns Hopkins University Press, 1979.

Voslensky, Michael. *Nomenklatura: Anatomy of the Soviet Ruling Class.* London: Bodley Head, 1984.

Walicki, Andrzej. *A History of Russian Thought: From the Enlightenment to Marxism.* Oxford: Clarendon Press, 1988.

Warner, Edward L. *The Military in Contemporary Soviet Politics.* New York: Praeger, 1977.

Weber, Max. *Economy and Society.* Berkeley: University of California Press, 1978.

———. *Essays in Sociology,* ed. H. H. Gerth, C. Wright Mills. New York: Oxford University Press, 1958.

———. "Socialism," in W. G. Runciman, ed., *Selection in Translations.* Cambridge: Cambridge University Press, 1978. Pp. 251–62.

———. *The Theory of Social and Economic Organization.* New York: Oxford University Press, 1947.

Wiatr, J. J., and A. Przeworski. "Control Without Opposition." *Government and Opposition* 1, no. 2 (1966).

Wilke, M., P. Erier, P. Goerner, P. Kubina, and H. P. Muller. *SED-Politburo und polnische Krise 1980/82,* vol. 1: *1980.* Berlin: Forschungsverbund SED-Staat, 1993.

Yakovlev, Alexander. *Perestroika: nadiezhdy i realnosti.* Moscow: Novosti, 1991.

Yeltsin, Boris. *Against the Grain: An Autobiography.* London: Pan Books, 1990.

———. *The View from the Kremlin.* London: HarperCollins, 1994.

Zalewski, Eugeniusz. *Planning Reforms in the Soviet Union, 1962–1966: An Analysis of Recent Trends in Economic Organization and Management.* Chapel Hill: University of North Carolina Press, 1967.

Zaslavsky, Victor. "Nationalism and Democratic Transition in Post-Communist Societies." *Daedalus,* Spring 1992. Pp. 97–121.

———. *The Neo-Stalinist State: Class, Ethnicity, and Consensus in Soviet Society.* 2nd ed. Armonk, N.Y.: Sharpe, 1994.

———. "Success and Collapse: Traditional Soviet National Policy," in Ian Bremmer and Ray Taras, *Nations and Politics in the Soviet Successor States.* Cambridge: Cambridge University Press, 1993. Pp. 29–42.

Zelikov, Philip, and Condolenza Rice. *Germany Unified and Europe Transformed: A Study in Statecraft.* Cambridge, Mass.: Harvard University Press, 1995.

Index

Orwell, George, 9
Outer empire, 6, 27

Party conference (1988), 79, 92,
94, 96
Party Congress: Twentieth (1956),
64, 125; Twenty-seventh (1986),
77; Twenty-eighth (the last,
1990), 5, 54–55
Party-military relations, 57–82
Party secretaries (regional), 15
Party-state relationship, 123–129
Patrimonial regression, theory of,
4, 40–41
Patronage network(s), 15, 48
Pavlov, Valentin, 20, 155
Peace of Westphalia, 145
Perestroika: accounts of, 4; and
the army, 6; and central planning, 4; compared to other
Russian revolutions, 50; as
economic necessity, 4; and economic policy, 39; failure of, 54;
its consequences, 5; its ideas,
23, 27, 29; main actors of, 4;
policies of, 4; as reconstruction
of central power, 34; as a state-
building enterprise, 34; winding
up of, 53
Personnel changes: in the military,
72–74; in the party, 44, 51
Pipes, Richard, 150
Poland, 47, 48, 55, 60, 146; and
postcommunist transition, 110;
Round Table, 96; Solidarity
crisis, 67–74
Politburo, 12; Brezhnev's, 20, 58;
East German, 47; Gorbachev's,
44, 54, 55, 77; Lenin's, 24; and
the military, 77; transcripts on
Solidarity crisis, 68, 69
Postcommunist societies, 114

Postcommunist transition/reform,
109, 110, 146
Post-Stalinist regime, 33, 59, 77,
122, 124, 125–127
Prague Spring, 24, 47
Pravda, 63
Presidential Cabinet, 52
Presidential Council, 31, 52, 81
Prussia, 146
Pryce-Jones, David, 11, 83, 95, 98
Pugo, Boris, 55

Rakowski, Mieczyslaw, 96
Regional economic councils, 40
Regional party leaders, 5, 41, 124;
and the military, 64–66, 67; and
the succession struggle, 46–47.
See also local/territorial leaders;
regional secretaries; republican
leaders
Regional secretaries, 43, 45, 47,
75, 125. *See also* Local/territorial
leaders; Regional party leaders;
Republican leaders
Remnick, David, 11, 25
Republican administration, purge
of, 38
Republican leaders, 33, 40, 113. *See
also* local/territorial leaders
Republican parliaments, 55
Revolution(s) from above: Gor-
bachev's and Stalin's compared,
51, 125, 136
Rice, Condolenza, 86–88, 93
Rokkan, Stein, 114
Romania, 47, 48
Romanov, Grigory, 34, 80
Russian Communist Party, 54
Russian culture, symbols of, 3
Russian Federation, 50
Russian government, 50, 53, 114
Russian parliament, 50
Russian revolutions, 49–50

Wisła Suraska is a research fellow at

the Adam Smith Research Centre in Warsaw and a

visiting fellow at the Department of Political Science,

European University in Florence.

Library of Congress Cataloging-in-Publication Data
Suraska, Wisła.
How the Soviet Union disappeared : an essay on the
causes of dissolution / Wisła Suraska.
p.   cm.
Includes bibliographical references and index.
ISBN 0-8223-2235-8 (cloth : alk. paper). —
ISBN 0-8223-2124-6 (pbk. : alk. paper)
1. Soviet Union—Politics and government—1985-1991.
I. Title.
DK288.S87   1998
947.085'4—dc21   98-18636